Freudian Psychology

-

The Comprehensive Guide

by

VIRUTI SATYAN SHIVAN

Masters in Clinical Psychology
(Major)

"In books, as in life, it's not the size or looks but

the content that matters."

Disclaimer: *The information in this book is for general information purposes only and is not professional advice. It's not a replacement for proper training, diagnosis, treatment, or guidance from qualified professionals. Although we've tried to ensure accuracy, there may be errors or omissions, so it's essential to consult experts in the relevant fields and independently verify information when needed.*

Table of Contents

Introduction

Welcome to a journey through the fascinating world of Freudian psychology. In this guide, we're going to unravel the mysteries of the mind as seen through the eyes of one of psychology's most influential and controversial figures, Sigmund Freud.

Freudian psychology isn't just about understanding complex theories; it's a voyage into the depths of human nature, exploring the hidden corners of our minds that influence our behavior, relationships, and even our dreams. Whether you're a student of psychology, a professional in the field, or simply curious about what makes people tick, this guide promises to enlighten, challenge, and entertain you.

In the pages that follow, we'll explore Freud's life, his groundbreaking theories, and how they've shaped our understanding of the human psyche. From the id, ego, and superego to the Oedipus complex and beyond, we'll delve into concepts that have become part of our everyday language and cultural fabric.

But this isn't just a textbook. Along the way, we'll infuse our exploration with real-life examples, thought-provoking exercises, and a touch of humor. Psychology, after all, is about people - messy, fascinating, unpredictable people. So, let's approach it with the curiosity, openness, and a bit of playfulness it deserves.

As we embark on this journey, remember: Freudian psychology is not just a set of theories. It's a lens through which to view the human experience, a way to understand ourselves and others more deeply. So, fasten your seatbelts, and let's dive into the intriguing world of Freudian psychology.

Chapter 1: The Foundations of Freudian Psychology

1.1. Sigmund Freud: Life and Legacy

Sigmund Freud, often hailed as the father of psychoanalysis, was a figure who profoundly changed the way we think about the human mind. Born in 1856 in what is now the Czech Republic, Freud's life was as fascinating as the theories he developed.

Freud's journey into the realm of psychology began in the medical field, where his early work focused on neurology. However, it was his foray into the uncharted territories of the unconscious mind that would cement his legacy. Freud's theories, often controversial, challenged the prevailing notions of the Victorian era and opened up a whole new world of understanding human behavior.

His life was marked by both triumphs and challenges. He lived through World War I, faced anti-Semitism, and eventually fled Nazi-occupied Austria to spend his final years in London. Despite these hardships, Freud remained dedicated to his work, continually revising his theories and exploring new ideas until his death in 1939.

Freud's legacy is a complex one. On one hand, he's credited with foundational contributions to our understanding of the unconscious, dreams, and the role of childhood experiences. His concepts of the id, ego, and superego, as well as defense mechanisms, are still discussed in psychology courses around the world. On the other hand, many of his ideas have been criticized and challenged by subsequent generations of psychologists and scholars.

Nevertheless, Freud's impact on psychology, culture, and even art and literature, is undeniable. He provided a new lens through which to view human behavior and mental processes, one that has influenced countless fields and sparked endless debates.

As we delve into the foundations of Freudian psychology, it's essential to remember that we're not just exploring a set of theories; we're exploring a revolutionary way of thinking about the mind, developed by a man whose ideas continue to resonate more than a century later. So, let's embark on this journey with an open mind, ready to question, learn, and perhaps even be a bit Freudian in our curiosity.

1.2. Overview of Psychoanalytic Theory

Psychoanalytic theory, the brainchild of Sigmund Freud, is like a thrilling novel that attempts to read the subconscious mind's narrative. At its core, it's about understanding the unseen forces that drive our thoughts, feelings, and behaviors. Imagine an iceberg: what you see above the water represents our conscious mind, but it's the massive structure beneath, the unconscious, where the real action happens.

The Unconscious Mind: Freud proposed that the unconscious mind is a reservoir of feelings, thoughts, urges, and memories that are outside of our conscious awareness. It's like a storage room where we keep our deepest desires and fears. Most of the contents of the unconscious are unacceptable or unpleasant, such as feelings of pain, anxiety, or conflict.

Dream Analysis: Freud called dreams the "royal road to the unconscious." He believed that analyzing dreams could provide a fascinating peek into the unconscious mind. In dreams, our unconscious desires and thoughts find an outlet in a symbolic form. It's like decoding a secret language to understand what's going on beneath the surface.

Freudian Slip: Ever said something you didn't mean to? According to Freud, these slips of the tongue aren't just random mistakes but meaningful revelations from our subconscious. They are like little windows that accidentally open up, giving us a brief view into our inner world.

Psychosexual Development: This controversial theory suggests that our childhood experiences, particularly related to pleasure and frustration, shape our adult personality. Freud divided this into stages: oral, anal, phallic, latency, and genital. Each stage represents a different challenge and a specific area of gratification.

Defense Mechanisms: Our psyche has a toolkit for dealing with reality and protecting itself from anxiety. These tools, or defense mechanisms, include denial, repression, projection, and more. They're like our mind's security guards, stepping in when things get too overwhelming.

The Id, Ego, and Superego: Freud described these as the three parts of our psychic apparatus. The id is all about basic instincts and desires; think of it as the 'pleasure principle.' The ego, governed by the 'reality principle,' tries to keep the id in check. It's like a mediator. The superego, representing our moral conscience, adds another layer of complexity, often clashing with the id's desires.

Transference: In psychoanalysis, transference is the process of projecting feelings about important people from one's past onto the therapist. It's like a rerun of old emotional conflicts, but with the therapist as a stand-in.

Psychoanalytic theory is not just a theory about mental illness; it's a comprehensive theory about human nature and behavior. It's an invitation to explore the depths of the human psyche, understanding that much of what drives us remains hidden in the shadows of our unconscious. As we continue our exploration, remember that these concepts aren't just abstract ideas; they're tools to help us understand the complexities of the human experience.

1.3. Key Principles of Freudian Thought

Freudian thought, with its intriguing blend of complexity and controversy, revolves around several key principles that form the bedrock of Freud's psychoanalytic theory. These principles, like the pieces of a puzzle, come together to offer a unique perspective on human psychology.

The Unconscious Mind: Imagine an iceberg floating in the ocean. The tip represents our conscious mind, the part we're aware of and can access easily. But beneath the waterline lies the vast expanse of the unconscious mind, filled with desires, thoughts, and memories beyond our conscious awareness. This hidden realm, according to Freud, is the powerhouse driving much of our behavior and emotional responses.

Psychosexual Development: This principle suggests that early childhood experiences, particularly those centered around pleasure-seeking instincts, play a crucial role in shaping our adult personality. Freud outlined five stages: oral, anal, phallic, latency, and genital. Each stage is associated with specific conflicts and potential fixations if these conflicts are not resolved adequately.

Oedipus Complex: One of Freud's most famous (and controversial) ideas is the Oedipus complex, occurring during the phallic stage of development. It posits that boys develop unconscious sexual desires for their mother and hostility towards their father, viewing him as a rival. In girls, this manifests as the Electra complex, with the feelings directed towards the father.

Dream Interpretation: Freud viewed dreams as the royal road to understanding the unconscious mind. He believed that dreams are filled with symbolic representations of unconscious desires and conflicts. Through the process of dream analysis, one can uncover the hidden meanings and underlying wishes that the conscious mind keeps at bay.

The Structure of Personality: Freud's model of the human psyche is divided into three parts: the id, ego, and superego. The id operates on the pleasure principle, seeking immediate gratification. The ego, governed by the reality principle, tries to mediate between the id's desires and the real world's demands. The superego, formed around the age of five, is the moral compass that guides the ego, often in conflict with the id's impulses.

Defense Mechanisms: The ego employs various defense mechanisms to cope with anxiety and prevent the conscious mind from being overwhelmed by unacceptable thoughts and feelings. These include repression (pushing thoughts into the unconscious), denial (refusing to acknowledge reality), projection (attributing one's own unacceptable feelings to others), and others.

Transference: In psychotherapy, transference refers to the phenomenon where patients project feelings and attitudes from a past relationship onto the therapist. This projection can reveal unresolved conflicts and feelings, providing a valuable tool for therapy.

Understanding these principles is like unlocking a door to the deeper layers of the human psyche. Freud's ideas, despite the controversies and debates they sparked, offer a fascinating lens through which we can view and understand human behavior, motivations, and the complexities of the mind. As we delve further into Freudian psychology, we'll see how these principles interweave and influence various aspects of human thought and behavior.

1.4. Exercise: 10 MCQs with Answers at the End

Engage with the foundational concepts of Freudian psychology through this set of multiple-choice questions. Test your understanding and recall of the key principles discussed in this chapter. Answers are provided at the end.

1. **Sigmund Freud is best known as the founder of:**

   A. Behaviorism

   B. Cognitive Psychology

   C. Psychoanalysis

D. Humanistic Psychology

2. The unconscious mind, according to Freud, primarily contains:

   A. Logical thoughts

   B. Conscious desires

   C. Repressed feelings and desires

   D. Immediate reactions to stimuli

3. In Freud's theory of psychosexual development, the first stage is:

   A. Anal

   B. Oral

   C. Phallic

   D. Latency

4. Freud's concept of the Oedipus complex is mainly associated with which psychosexual stage?

   A. Genital

   B. Oral

   C. Phallic

   D. Latency

5. Which part of the human psyche operates on the 'pleasure principle' according to Freud?

A. Ego

B. Superego

C. Id

D. Conscious Mind

6. Freud's method of analyzing dreams to understand the unconscious is known as:

A. Free association

B. Hypnotherapy

C. Dream interpretation

D. Transference

7. A Freudian slip is believed to reveal:

A. Logical errors in thinking

B. Unconscious thoughts and desires

C. Errors in language processing

D. Misunderstood words or phrases

8. **Which of the following is a defense mechanism according to Freudian theory?**

   A. Rationalization

   B. Introspection

   C. Empathy

   D. Mindfulness

9. **The 'reality principle' is associated with which component of the psyche?**

   A. Id

   B. Ego

   C. Superego

   D. Conscious Mind

10. **Transference in psychoanalytic therapy refers to:**

   A. Transfer of skills from therapist to client

   B. Projecting feelings about others onto the therapist

   C. Changing therapists frequently

   D. Transferring from one type of therapy to another

Answers:

1. C. Psychoanalysis

2. C. Repressed feelings and desires

3. B. Oral

4. C. Phallic

5. C. Id

6. C. Dream interpretation

7. B. Unconscious thoughts and desires

8. A. Rationalization

9. B. Ego

10. B. Projecting feelings about others onto the therapist

This exercise is designed to reinforce your understanding of Freudian psychology's fundamental concepts. Reflect on these questions to deepen your comprehension and appreciation of the intricacies of Freud's theories.

Chapter 2: The Structure of the Mind

2.1. The Conscious, Preconscious, and Unconscious

Delving into the structure of the mind according to Freudian psychology is like exploring an intricate mansion with various hidden rooms and passages. Freud conceptualized the mind as being divided into three distinct regions: the conscious, preconscious, and unconscious. Each of these regions plays a crucial role in shaping our thoughts, behaviors, and overall personality.

The Conscious Mind: This is the part of the mind that we are aware of, the 'living room' of our mental mansion, if you will. It includes everything we are thinking of at a given moment: our present perceptions, memories, thoughts, fantasies, and feelings. It's like the spotlight on a stage, illuminating specific content but not the entire scene.

The Preconscious Mind: Imagine a library filled with books. The preconscious mind is similar to this library. It contains all the information that you are not currently thinking about, but can easily retrieve and bring into conscious awareness. It's like the bookshelf of your mind, holding your available knowledge, memories, stored information, and experiences that can be readily accessed.

The Unconscious Mind: Now, let's venture into the basement of our mansion, a place that's out of sight but incredibly influential. The unconscious mind is a reservoir of feelings, thoughts, urges, and memories that are outside of our conscious awareness. Most of this content is unacceptable or unpleasant, such as feelings of pain, anxiety, or conflict. This part of the mind is difficult to access and is kept out of conscious awareness by defense mechanisms. However, these unconscious thoughts and feelings can sometimes slip into our conscious mind, often through dreams or Freudian slips.

Understanding the interplay between these three regions is key to grasping Freudian psychology. The conscious mind governs our daily functions and decision-making processes. The preconscious stores information that can be brought into consciousness upon need. And the mysterious unconscious holds our deepest desires and fears, exerting a profound influence on our thoughts and behaviors without us even realizing it.

The dynamics of these three layers of the mind create a fascinating landscape of human psychology, where much of what drives us remains hidden, yet powerfully influential. It's a landscape that Freud invited us to explore, to better understand ourselves and others. As we continue to navigate through the depths of Freudian thought, remember that the mind's structure is complex, layered, and endlessly intriguing.

2.2. The Id, Ego, and Superego

In Freudian psychology, the psyche is not just a single entity but a dynamic system of three parts: the id, ego, and superego. These three elements interact in fascinating ways to form our behavior, decisions, and personality. Let's explore each of these components, akin to characters in the drama of the mind.

The Id: Picture a newborn baby — all impulse and desire. This is the id in action. The id is the most primitive part of our psyche, present from birth. It operates solely on the pleasure principle, seeking immediate gratification for our basic needs and desires. The id is unconscious and impulsive. It doesn't think about consequences or social appropriateness. It just wants what it wants, when it wants it.

The Ego: Now, imagine growing up and learning that you can't always get what you want, when you want it. That's where the ego comes in. The ego is the decision-making component of the personality, operating on the reality principle. It mediates between the desires of the id and the constraints of the external world. The ego is like a skilled negotiator, balancing instinctual needs with social norms and expectations. It's the rational part of our psyche, responsible for logical thinking and planning.

The Superego: Enter the superego, which develops around the age of five. This component represents the moral standards and ideals we acquire from our parents and society. It's the ethical part of our personality, providing guidelines for making judgments. The superego can be seen as the critical and moralizing function. It strives for perfection, not pleasure, and it works to suppress the urges of the id and persuade the ego to turn to moralistic goals rather than simply realistic ones.

The dynamic interplay between the id, ego, and superego shapes our behavior and personality. The ego constantly works to balance the demands of the id and the superego, often leading to internal conflicts. For example, the id may demand immediate satisfaction, the superego may oppose it on moral grounds, and the ego must find a realistic and socially acceptable way to satisfy both.

Understanding these three aspects of the psyche is crucial in Freudian psychology. They represent the key forces that drive our actions and influence our mental health. As we navigate through our daily lives, the id, ego, and superego are continuously at play, guiding our decisions, shaping our interactions, and contributing to the unique individuals we are.

2.3. Dynamics of the Psyche

The dynamics of the psyche in Freudian psychology are like the intricate workings of a complex machine, where different parts interact and influence each other to produce a functioning whole. In understanding the psyche's dynamics, we explore how the conscious, preconscious, and unconscious minds, along with the id, ego, and superego, interact to shape our thoughts, feelings, and behaviors.

Interaction Between the Conscious, Preconscious, and Unconscious: The psyche's three levels are in constant interaction. The conscious mind is where we spend most of our waking hours, but it's continually influenced by the preconscious and unconscious. Ideas and memories from the preconscious can easily pop into our conscious mind. The unconscious, however, is a bit more elusive. It holds desires and memories that are generally inaccessible to the conscious mind but can surface in disguised forms, such as dreams or Freudian slips.

The Conflict Between Id, Ego, and Superego: Picture the psyche as a battleground where the id, ego, and superego are constantly in conflict. The Id seeks immediate gratification, the superego aims for moral perfection, and the ego is caught in the middle, trying to please both while dealing with reality. This conflict can lead to anxiety, which the ego tries to reduce through various defense mechanisms.

Role of Defense Mechanisms: Defense mechanisms are psychological strategies used by the ego to manage stress and reduce anxiety caused by internal conflicts. These mechanisms, such as repression, denial, and projection, operate unconsciously and help the ego keep the peace between the id and superego. While these mechanisms can be helpful, overreliance on them may lead to unhealthy behaviors and mental health issues.

Anxiety and Neurosis: Freud believed that anxiety is the result of conflicts between the id, ego, and superego. This anxiety can manifest in various forms of neurosis, depending on how the ego defends against these internal conflicts. For instance, an overactive superego might lead to feelings of guilt and inferiority, while an unchecked id might result in impulsive and self-destructive behaviors.

Resolution of Conflicts: In psychoanalysis, the goal is to bring unconscious conflicts to conscious awareness. By doing so, an individual can work through these conflicts, understand their origins, and find healthier ways to resolve them. This process often involves exploring past experiences, understanding dream symbolism, and analyzing the transference relationship in therapy.

Understanding the dynamics of the psyche is crucial in grasping Freudian psychology. It's a field that goes beyond mere academic interest; it's about understanding the deep-rooted forces that drive us as individuals. By exploring these dynamics, we gain insights into our behavior and can work towards a more balanced and psychologically healthy life.

2.4. Exercise: 10 MCQs with Answers at the End

Let's reinforce your understanding of the concepts discussed in Chapter 2 with a set of multiple-choice questions. Test your knowledge of the structure of the mind and the dynamics within it according to Freudian psychology. Answers are provided at the end.

1. **Which part of the mind is in constant contact with the needs of the body according to Freud?**

    A. Conscious

    B. Preconscious

    C. Unconscious

    D. Id

2. **The preconscious is like:**

    A. A locked safe

    B. A stage spotlight

    C. A library

    D. An iceberg under water

3. **According to Freud, the ego operates on the:**

    A. Pleasure Principle

    B. Reality Principle

    C. Morality Principle

    D. Anxiety Principle

4. **The superego is primarily concerned with:**

    A. Immediate gratification

    B. Social norms and morals

    C. Instinctual desires

D. Rational thinking

5. Which of the following best describes the unconscious mind?

A. Part of the mind that contains all our thoughts and memories

B. The region of the mind that arranges thoughts logically

C. A reservoir of feelings and thoughts that are inaccessible to consciousness

D. The part of the mind that deals with the external world

6. Anxiety in Freud's psychoanalytic theory is most often due to:

A. External threats

B. Conflicts between the id, ego, and superego

C. Lack of knowledge

D. Poor decision-making skills

7. Which defense mechanism involves refusing to accept reality?

A. Repression

B. Denial

C. Projection

D. Rationalization

8. **The Oedipus complex is resolved during which of Freud's psychosexual stages?**

   A. Oral

   B. Anal

   C. Phallic

   D. Latency

9. **In Freud's model of the psyche, the id is:**

   A. Fully conscious

   B. Partially conscious

   C. Unconscious

   D. Preconscious

10. **The main purpose of Freudian defense mechanisms is to:**

   A. Strengthen the superego

   B. Balance the id and the ego

   C. Reduce anxiety and protect the ego

   D. Increase consciousness of hidden desires

Answers:

1. D. Id

2. C. A library

3. B. Reality Principle

4. B. Social norms and morals

5. C. A reservoir of feelings and thoughts that are inaccessible to consciousness

6. B. Conflicts between the id, ego, and superego

7. B. Denial

8. C. Phallic

9. C. Unconscious

10. C. Reduce anxiety and protect the ego

This exercise is designed to deepen your understanding of the complex structure and dynamics of the mind in Freudian psychology. By reflecting on these questions, you can gain a better grasp of the intricate interplay of conscious, preconscious, and unconscious realms, as well as the roles of the id, ego, and superego.

Chapter 3: Psychosexual Development

3.1. Stages of Psychosexual Development

Freud's theory of psychosexual development is one of the most intriguing and debated aspects of his work. It suggests that our personality develops through a series of stages during childhood, each characterized by different ways of obtaining pleasure. According to Freud, if these stages are not resolved properly, it can lead to fixation and impact adult personality. Let's explore these fascinating stages.

1. **The Oral Stage (0-1 years):** This is the first stage of psychosexual development, occurring from birth to about 18 months. During this stage, pleasure is centered around the mouth. Activities like sucking and biting are vital for the infant's pleasure and stimulation. Fixation at this stage may result in issues such as dependency or aggression in adulthood.

2. **The Anal Stage (1-3 years):** As the child grows, the focus of pleasure shifts from the mouth to the anus. This stage is associated with the control of bowel and bladder movements. The primary conflict at this stage is toilet training, and how it's handled by caregivers can impact the child's future personality.

A too strict approach can lead to an obsessive-compulsive personality, while a too lenient approach can lead to a messy or destructive personality.

3. **The Phallic Stage (3-6 years):** In this stage, the focus of pleasure is the genitals. Freud introduced the Oedipus complex for boys and the Electra complex for girls, where children develop unconscious sexual desires towards the opposite-sex parent and hostility towards the same-sex parent. Resolution of these complexes is crucial for healthy psychological development.

4. **The Latency Stage (6-puberty):** This stage is a bit of a breather in the psychosexual stages. Sexual impulses are repressed, allowing the child to focus on developing social skills, friendships, and acquiring knowledge. This stage is crucial for developing social and communication skills.

5. **The Genital Stage (puberty onwards):** The final stage of psychosexual development begins with puberty. It's a time of sexual reawakening where the focus of pleasure shifts to the genitals. Unlike the phallic stage, the pleasure is sought through relationships with others. If previous stages have been successfully resolved, the individual should emerge as a well-rounded, sexually mature adult.

Understanding these stages gives us a window into Freud's view of human development and the complex interplay of psychological forces that shape our adult personality. While modern psychology may view some aspects of Freud's theory as outdated or controversial, its influence on our understanding of human development is undeniable. As we explore these stages, remember they are part of a theory that, despite its controversies, has had a profound impact on both psychology and popular culture.

3.2. Implications of Developmental Stages

Freud's stages of psychosexual development, beyond their immediate framework, offer deep implications for understanding human behavior and personality development. The way individuals navigate these stages, according to Freud, has a lasting impact on their adult lives. Let's delve into the implications of each stage and how they potentially shape us.

1. **Implications of the Oral Stage:** If a child's needs are not adequately met during the oral stage, or if oral stimulation is either under or over-gratified, this can lead to what Freud termed an 'oral fixation.' In adulthood, this may manifest as behaviors centered around the mouth, like smoking, overeating, or excessive talking. On a psychological level, such individuals might struggle with dependency or aggression.

2. **Implications of the Anal Stage:** The anal stage is closely tied to a child's experience with toilet training. Freud suggested that how parents handle toilet training can greatly influence a person's personality. A too strict approach might lead to an anal-retentive personality, characterized by obsessiveness, tidiness,

punctuality, and respect for authority. Conversely, a too lenient approach might result in an anal-expulsive personality, characterized by messiness, recklessness, and defiant behavior.

3. **Implications of the Phallic Stage:** The resolution of the Oedipus and Electra complexes during the phallic stage is crucial for healthy psychosexual development. Unresolved complexes could lead to a fixation that manifests in adulthood as difficulty in forming healthy romantic relationships, a tendency towards vanity or self-obsession, or even sexual dysfunctions.

4. **Implications of the Latency Stage:** While less directly impactful in terms of specific fixations, the latency stage is crucial for developing social and communication skills. Success in this stage leads to the ability to form healthy relationships with peers and a strong sense of identity and competence.

5. **Implications of the Genital Stage:** Successfully navigating this stage depends largely on resolving the conflicts and fixations of previous stages. If earlier issues are unresolved, they might resurface and affect the individual's ability to form mature, reciprocal relationships. In a broader sense, this stage is about achieving balance and wholeness in one's personality.

Freud's theory, while foundational, is not without its critics. Many modern psychologists argue that development is a more continuous process and is influenced by a wider range of factors than Freud suggested. Nonetheless, understanding these stages and their implications provides valuable insight into the complexities of human behavior and personality. Freud's ideas continue to spark discussion and debate, highlighting the enduring nature of his influence on the field of psychology.

3.3. Critique and Modern Perspectives

While Freud's theory of psychosexual development was groundbreaking and influential, it has not been without its fair share of criticism and alternative viewpoints in modern psychology. Let's explore some key critiques and how contemporary perspectives have evolved our understanding of human development.

Critiques of Freud's Theory:

1. **Lack of Empirical Evidence:** One of the primary criticisms of Freud's psychosexual theory is the lack of empirical evidence supporting it. Much of Freud's work was based on case studies and not on broad, systematic research, leading many to question the generalizability of his conclusions.

2. **Overemphasis on Sexuality:** Freud's theory heavily focuses on sexuality as the primary driver of personality development. Critics argue that this overemphasis neglects other crucial factors such as social, cultural, and environmental influences.

3. **Gender Bias:** Freud's theory has been criticized for perpetuating gender stereotypes, particularly in his descriptions of the Oedipus and Electra complexes. His views on female

psychology and development were often seen as limited and biased.

4. **Deterministic Nature:** Freud's theory suggests that personality is largely shaped by experiences in early childhood, implying a deterministic view of development. Critics argue that this overlooks the ongoing developmental processes and changes that can occur throughout life.

Modern Perspectives:

1. **Greater Emphasis on Social and Cultural Factors:** Contemporary theories of development place more emphasis on the roles of social, cultural, and environmental factors in shaping personality. This includes the influence of family, peers, education, and broader societal norms.

2. **Attachment Theory:** Modern psychology has seen the rise of attachment theory, which focuses on the importance of the relationship between a child and their primary caregiver. This theory suggests that secure attachment in early life leads to healthier psychological development.

3. **Continual Development:** Modern theories often view development as a lifelong process, where personality and behavior can change and evolve over time. This perspective contrasts with Freud's more static view of personality being cemented in early childhood.

4. **Neuroscientific Approaches:** Advances in neuroscience have provided more insight into brain development and its correlation with behavior and personality. This research often challenges or refines psychoanalytic theories with empirical data.

In summary, while Freud's theory of psychosexual development has been foundational in the field of psychology, it is just one perspective among many. Modern psychology has expanded and evolved these ideas, offering a more holistic and nuanced understanding of human development. The critiques and ongoing research in psychology demonstrate the dynamic nature of the field, always growing and adapting in light of new knowledge and perspectives.

3.4. Exercise: 10 MCQs with Answers at the End

Test your understanding of Freud's psychosexual development theory with these multiple-choice questions. This exercise will help reinforce key concepts and critiques discussed in Chapter 3. The answers are provided at the end.

1. **During which stage of Freud's psychosexual development does the Oedipus complex occur?**

   A. Oral

   B. Anal

   C. Phallic

D. Latency

2. **Which stage of psychosexual development is characterized by the formation of social and communication skills?**

A. Oral

B. Anal

C. Latency

D. Genital

3. **An overly strict toilet training during the anal stage may lead to an adult personality that is:**

A. Dependent

B. Obsessive-compulsive

C. Narcissistic

D. Socially withdrawn

4. **Freud's psychosexual development theory has been criticized for its:**

A. Underemphasis on sexual themes

B. Lack of empirical evidence

C. Focus on late childhood experiences

D. Emphasis on conscious thought processes

5. **According to Freud, unresolved conflicts in the phallic stage may lead to:**

A. Intellectual disabilities

B. Difficulty in forming healthy romantic relationships

C. Poor social skills

D. Lack of moral development

6. **What is the primary focus of the genital stage in Freud's theory?**

A. Developing basic trust

B. Mastering toilet training

C. Forming mature, reciprocal relationships

D. Resolving the Oedipus complex

7. **Which modern theory places importance on the child-caregiver relationship, contrasting Freud's emphasis on psychosexual stages?**

A. Cognitive Development Theory

B. Behaviorism

C. Attachment Theory

D. Social Learning Theory

8. **What did Freud suggest is largely completed during the latency stage of psychosexual development?**

A. Sexual identification

B. Repression of aggressive impulses

C. Development of defense mechanisms

D. Social and communication skills

9. Critics of Freud's theory argue that personality development:

A. Stops after adolescence

B. Is only influenced by sexual factors

C. Continues throughout life

D. Is solely determined by early childhood experiences

10. An example of gender bias in Freud's theory is seen in his concept of:

A. The unconscious mind

B. Defense mechanisms

C. The Electra complex

D. The reality principle

Answers:

1. C. Phallic

2. C. Latency

3. B. Obsessive-compulsive

4. B. Lack of empirical evidence

5. B. Difficulty in forming healthy romantic relationships

6. C. Forming mature, reciprocal relationships

7. C. Attachment Theory

8. D. Social and communication skills

9. C. Continues throughout life

10. C. The Electra complex

This exercise is designed to deepen your understanding of Freud's psychosexual development stages and their implications, as well as the critiques and modern perspectives that have emerged in response to Freud's theory. Reflecting on these questions can enhance your comprehension of the complexities of human development as viewed through the lens of Freudian psychology.

Chapter 4: Dream Analysis

4.1. The Role of Dreams in Psychoanalysis

In the realm of Freudian psychology, dreams hold a place of utmost significance. Freud famously referred to them as the "royal road to the unconscious," a pathway to the deepest, often unacknowledged, parts of ourselves. Let's explore the fascinating role dreams play in psychoanalysis.

Window to the Unconscious: Freud believed that dreams are a manifestation of our unconscious desires, fears, and conflicts. While our conscious mind rests during sleep, the unconscious mind is at its most active. Dreams, in this sense, are like coded messages from the unconscious, offering insights into our internal world that might be inaccessible or too threatening to face directly when awake.

Dream Work: Freud introduced the concept of 'dream work,' a process through which the content of the unconscious mind is transformed into the symbolic language of dreams. This process involves mechanisms like condensation (combining multiple ideas into one symbol), displacement (shifting emotional significance from one idea to another), and symbolism (using objects or events to represent unconscious thoughts).

Manifest and Latent Content: Freud differentiated between the manifest content of a dream (what the dream appears to be about on the surface) and its latent content (the hidden psychological meaning). For example, dreaming about flying might not just be about flying (manifest content) but could represent a desire for freedom or escape from constraints (latent content).

Therapeutic Importance: In psychoanalysis, dream analysis is a vital therapeutic tool. It allows the therapist and the patient to uncover and interpret the latent content of dreams, thus gaining insight into unresolved issues and hidden desires. By analyzing dreams, patients can work through their unconscious conflicts, leading to greater self-awareness and psychological healing.

Contemporary Views: While Freud's theories on dreams were revolutionary, they have been met with skepticism and modification over time. Contemporary psychologists view dreams as a complex interplay of neurological, cognitive, and psychological factors. Modern research in sleep and dream science has expanded our understanding, though the symbolic and interpretative analysis of dreams still finds relevance in various therapeutic contexts.

Dreams, in Freudian psychoanalysis, are not just nightly distractions but meaningful, symbolic narratives that tell the story of our inner selves. They offer a unique and invaluable perspective on our unconscious mind, providing a rich source of material for understanding and resolving deep-seated psychological conflicts.

4.2. Dream Symbolism and Interpretation

Freud's exploration into the world of dreams opened up a fascinating avenue for understanding the unconscious mind. In psychoanalysis, dreams are not just random images; they are laden with symbolism, each element carrying a deeper meaning related to the dreamer's life. Let's dive into the intriguing process of dream symbolism and interpretation in Freudian psychology.

Understanding Dream Symbolism:

1. **Universal Symbols:** Freud believed that certain dream symbols have universal meanings. For instance, kings and queens might represent the dreamer's parents, while ascending a staircase could symbolize sexual intercourse. However, Freud also cautioned that the interpretation of these symbols can vary significantly depending on the individual's experiences and feelings.

2. **Personal Symbols:** In addition to universal symbols, dreams also contain personal symbols that have unique meanings specific to the individual. These symbols are shaped by the dreamer's experiences, relationships, and emotional state. For example, dreaming about a particular house might represent a specific period or aspect of the dreamer's life.

3. **The Role of Context:** The context in which a symbol appears in a dream is crucial for its interpretation. A symbol's meaning can

change based on the other elements present in the dream and the emotions associated with it. For instance, water might symbolize purification in one context but could represent emotional turmoil in another.

The Process of Interpretation:

1. **Free Association:** One key method used in dream interpretation is free association. This involves the dreamer describing the dream and then freely expressing any thoughts, memories, or feelings that each element of the dream evokes. This process helps uncover the hidden, latent content of the dream.

2. **Exploring the Latent Content:** The latent content of a dream, according to Freud, is the hidden psychological meaning behind the dream's manifest content (the literal storyline). Interpretation involves delving into the latent content to reveal the unconscious desires, fears, and conflicts symbolized in the dream.

3. **Therapeutic Dialogue:** Dream interpretation is not a solo endeavor; it is part of a therapeutic dialogue between the analyst and the patient. The analyst helps guide the patient through the interpretation, providing insights but also allowing the patient to discover personal meanings and connections.

Contemporary Views on Dream Interpretation:

While Freud's approach to dream interpretation remains influential, contemporary psychology offers a more diverse perspective. Some modern theories suggest that dreams help in emotional regulation, problem-solving, or are simply a byproduct of brain activity during sleep. However, many therapists still incorporate elements of Freud's dream analysis into their practice, recognizing the value of dreams in gaining insight into a patient's subconscious mind.

In Freudian psychology, dream interpretation is a unique and powerful tool for unlocking the mysteries of the unconscious mind. It provides a creative and insightful pathway to understanding our deepest fears, desires, and unresolved conflicts, making it an invaluable component of psychoanalytic therapy.

4.3. Case Studies in Dream Analysis

Dream analysis has always been an integral part of Freudian psychoanalysis, providing fascinating insights into the unconscious mind. By examining specific case studies, we can better understand how Freud used dream analysis to uncover hidden desires and conflicts. Let's delve into a couple of illustrative cases that highlight the process and significance of dream analysis in psychoanalytic therapy.

Case Study 1: The Wolf Man

One of Freud's most famous case studies involved a patient dubbed the "Wolf Man," who suffered from a phobia of wolves. Through dream analysis, Freud explored a dream the Wolf Man had as a child, where he saw a group of white wolves sitting in a tree outside his window. Freud interpreted this dream as a manifestation of the patient's repressed fears and desires related to his father. The wolves represented a distorted version of a childhood memory involving his father, symbolizing both fear and admiration. This case exemplified how early childhood experiences and familial relationships could manifest in dreams, influencing later emotional and psychological issues.

Case Study 2: Dora

Another notable case was that of "Dora," a young woman experiencing hysteria. Freud analyzed several of her dreams, including one where she rescued her father from a fire. Freud interpreted this dream as reflecting Dora's mixed feelings of resentment and affection towards her father, as well as unresolved Oedipal conflicts. Through the analysis of this and other dreams, Freud uncovered deep-seated issues regarding Dora's family dynamics and her struggles with her own identity and relationships.

Insights from Case Studies:

1. **Uncovering Repressed Emotions:** These case studies illustrate how dreams can act as windows to repressed emotions and unresolved conflicts, often rooted in early childhood experiences and family relationships.

2. **Symbolic Representation:** They demonstrate the symbolic nature of dreams, where real-life concerns and experiences are transformed into a metaphorical language that can be decoded through analysis.

3. **The Therapeutic Process:** These cases also highlight the therapeutic process in psychoanalysis, where the therapist guides the patient in exploring and interpreting their dreams to gain insights into their unconscious mind.

4. **Personal and Universal Themes:** Both cases show how dreams can contain both personal symbols (unique to the individual) and universal symbols (common across different people), and how the interpretation of these symbols can provide profound insights into the patient's psyche.

5. **Critiques and Evolution:** While these case studies are seminal in the field of psychoanalysis, modern psychology views them with some skepticism, especially regarding Freud's emphasis on sexual themes and the subjective nature of dream interpretation. Contemporary approaches to dream analysis often incorporate a broader range of psychological theories and emphasize the dreamer's own perspective and experience.

These case studies from Freudian psychoanalysis not only demonstrate the complex relationship between dreams and the unconscious mind but also show how dream analysis can be a powerful tool in understanding and resolving deep-seated psychological issues. They remain a testament to the enduring legacy of Freud's work in psychoanalysis and dream interpretation.

4.4. Exercise: 10 MCQs with Answers at the End

Enhance your understanding of Freud's dream analysis with these multiple-choice questions. These questions cover key concepts and ideas presented in Chapter 4. Answers are provided at the end for you to check your understanding.

1. **Freud referred to dreams as:**

   A. The royal road to the unconscious

   B. A meaningless byproduct of sleep

   C. The conscious mind's playground

   D. A reflection of daily activities

2. **In dream analysis, the manifest content refers to:**

   A. The hidden psychological meaning of the dream

   B. The literal storyline of the dream

   C. The dreamer's conscious experience

   D. The dreamer's repressed memories

3. **The process of transforming the unconscious thoughts into the symbolic language of dreams is known as:**

A. Dream translation

B. Dream work

C. Dream interpretation

D. Dream conversion

4. **Which of the following is a mechanism used in dream work?**

A. Rationalization

B. Displacement

C. Sublimation

D. Regression

5. **According to Freud, a dream about climbing a staircase might symbolically represent:**

A. A journey to success

B. Sexual intercourse

C. A desire for higher knowledge

D. Escaping from reality

6. **Which method is primarily used in Freudian dream interpretation?**

A. Hypnosis

B. Free association

C. Cognitive restructuring

D. Behavioral analysis

7. **In Freudian dream analysis, latent content is:**

A. Easily understandable and clear

B. The superficial aspect of the dream

C. The hidden psychological meaning of the dream

D. The remembered story of the dream

8. **Freud's analysis of the 'Wolf Man' focused on:**

A. The man's fear of animals

B. Repressed memories of childhood

C. A dream about a group of wolves

D. The man's relationship with his mother

9. **Which of these is a contemporary critique of Freud's dream analysis?**

   A. Overemphasis on sleep quality

   B. Excessive focus on sexual themes

   C. Ignoring the role of nightmares

   D. Underestimating the role of conscious thought

10. **Dream analysis in psychoanalysis is primarily used for:**

   A. Entertainment purposes

   B. Uncovering unconscious desires and conflicts

   C. Predicting future events

   D. Improving sleep quality

Answers:

1. A. The royal road to the unconscious

2. B. The literal storyline of the dream

3. B. Dream work

4. B. Displacement

5. B. Sexual intercourse

6. B. Free association

7. C. The hidden psychological meaning of the dream

8. C. A dream about a group of wolves

9. B. Excessive focus on sexual themes

10. B. Uncovering unconscious desires and conflicts

These questions are designed to deepen your grasp of the complex and insightful world of Freudian dream analysis. Reflect on how dreams can reveal much about our unconscious mind and the integral role they play in psychoanalytic therapy.

Chapter 5: Defense Mechanisms

5.1. Understanding Defense Mechanisms

In Freudian psychology, defense mechanisms are psychological strategies employed by the unconscious mind to manipulate, deny, or distort reality in order to defend against feelings of anxiety and unacceptable impulses and to maintain one's self-schema. These mechanisms are not used deliberately but happen automatically and unconsciously. Let's dive into the world of defense mechanisms and understand their role in our psyche.

The Nature of Defense Mechanisms:

1. **Unconscious Processes:** Defense mechanisms operate at an unconscious level and help an individual cope with reality and maintain self-image. They are natural and normal, and everyone uses them to some extent.

2. **Protection Against Anxiety:** The primary function of defense mechanisms is to protect the mind from anxiety and social sanctions and/or to provide a refuge from a situation with which one cannot currently cope.

3. **Balance Between Id, Ego, and Superego:** Defense mechanisms are primarily used by the ego to deal with conflict between the id (instinctual needs and desires) and the superego (moral and ethical codes).

Common Defense Mechanisms:

1. **Repression:** Keeping distressing thoughts and feelings buried in the unconscious. For example, a person who has repressed memories of abuse suffered as a child may later have difficulty forming relationships.

2. **Denial:** Refusing to acknowledge some painful aspect of external reality or subjective experience that would be apparent to others. An example is a partner denying the evidence of his loved one's affair.

3. **Projection:** Attributing one's own unacceptable feelings and impulses to someone else. For instance, a person who is aggressive might accuse other people of being aggressive towards them.

4. **Rationalization:** Justifying one's behaviors and motivations by substituting "good," acceptable reasons for these motivations. For example, a student who blames a poor exam score on the difficulty of the questions rather than their lack of study.

5. **Displacement:** Shifting sexual or aggressive impulses to a more acceptable or less threatening target. This occurs when a person feels angry towards their boss but instead expresses anger towards their spouse or children.

6. **Sublimation:** Channeling unacceptable impulses into socially acceptable activities. For example, someone with aggressive tendencies becomes a professional fighter.

7. **Regression:** Reverting to an earlier stage of development in the face of unacceptable thoughts or impulses. For example, an adult throwing a temper tantrum when they don't get their way.

Understanding defense mechanisms provides insight into how individuals cope with reality and maintain their self-esteem. While these mechanisms can often help in coping with stress and anxiety, overreliance on them can lead to unhealthy patterns of behavior and emotional functioning. As such, recognizing and understanding these mechanisms can be an important aspect of psychotherapy and personal development.

5.2. Types and Functions of Defense Mechanisms

Defense mechanisms are psychological strategies used by the unconscious mind to manage stress, anxiety, and internal conflict. These mechanisms, which vary widely in their effectiveness and adaptiveness, serve several functions, from protecting the ego to maintaining psychological homeostasis. Let's explore some key types of defense mechanisms and their respective functions.

1. Repression:

- **Type:** Primitive

- **Function:** Keeps disturbing or threatening thoughts from becoming conscious.

- **Example:** An individual who experienced traumatic events in childhood might have no recollection of the events but still have emotional difficulties due to these repressed memories.

2. Denial:

- **Type:** Primitive

- **Function:** Refusing to accept external reality because it is too threatening; arguing against an anxiety-provoking stimulus by stating it doesn't exist.

- **Example:** A person who is a heavy smoker denies the evidence linking smoking to lung cancer as a way to continue smoking.

3. Projection:

- **Type:** Primitive

- **Function:** Attributing one's own unacceptable feelings and impulses to someone else.

- **Example:** A spouse who is unfaithful suspects their partner is being unfaithful.

4. Displacement:

- **Type:** Less primitive, more mature

- **Function:** Redirecting emotions to a substitute target.

- **Example:** A person who is frustrated by their boss at work may go home and kick the dog or start an argument with their family.

5. Intellectualization:

- **Type:** Intermediate

- **Function:** Avoiding unacceptable emotions by focusing on the intellectual aspects.

- **Example:** Focusing on the details of a funeral as opposed to the sadness and grief.

6. Rationalization:

- **Type:** Intermediate

- **Function:** Offering a different explanation for one's perceptions or behaviors in the face of a changing reality.

- **Example:** A student who justifies getting a poor grade by saying the exam was not important.

7. Regression:

  - **Type:** Primitive

  - **Function:** Temporarily reverting to a previous stage of development.

  - **Example:** An adult throwing a temper tantrum when they don't get their way.

8. Sublimation:

  - **Type:** Mature

  - **Function:** Channeling unacceptable impulses into socially acceptable activities.

  - **Example:** A person with aggressive urges becomes a surgeon.

9. Reaction Formation:

  - **Type:** Intermediate

  - **Function:** Reducing anxiety by adopting beliefs contrary to your own beliefs.

  - **Example:** A person who is angry with a colleague actually ends up being overly nice to them.

Each defense mechanism functions in its own way to help individuals cope with stress and anxiety. While some of these mechanisms might be considered more mature or adaptive than others, they all play a role in the complex dance of the human psyche. Understanding these mechanisms can lead to greater self-awareness and, in a therapeutic context, can help individuals work through their underlying issues and develop healthier coping strategies.

5.3. Defense Mechanisms in Everyday Life

Defense mechanisms are not just concepts found in psychology textbooks; they are active parts of our everyday lives, helping us cope with stress, protect our self-esteem, and maintain emotional equilibrium. While everyone uses defense mechanisms, the frequency and manner in which they are employed can vary greatly among individuals. Let's explore how these mechanisms manifest in common, day-to-day situations.

1. **Repression in Relationships:** Perhaps you've had a falling out with a friend years ago, but you can't recall the exact details. This might be repression at work, where your mind has pushed the painful memories out of conscious awareness to protect you from emotional distress.

2. **Denial in Health Issues:** Consider someone who has received a serious medical diagnosis but insists that there must be a mistake. They go about their life as if nothing has changed. This denial can be a way of avoiding the anxiety and fear associated with the illness.

3. **Projection in the Workplace:** Imagine a colleague who is always accusing others of being lazy and unproductive, yet they themselves often miss deadlines. They may be projecting their own shortcomings onto others to avoid facing their inadequacies.

4. **Displacement in Family Dynamics:** After a stressful day at work, a parent may become unusually irritable with their children or spouse. This displacement shifts the emotional frustration from the source (work) to a safer target (family).

5. **Intellectualization During Grief:** Someone who has lost a loved one might focus obsessively on the details of funeral arrangements, legal matters, etc., as a way of distancing themselves from the painful emotions of loss.

6. **Rationalization in Academic or Professional Setbacks:** A student who rationalizes a poor grade by claiming that the test was unfair is using this defense mechanism to protect their self-esteem.

7. **Regression Under Stress:** An adult might exhibit childish behavior, like whining or sulking, when under significant stress, reverting to behaviors from an earlier stage of development.

8. **Sublimation in Creative Pursuits:** An individual with aggressive tendencies might channel this energy into something constructive, like sports or art, turning potentially harmful impulses into productive activities.

9. **Reaction Formation in Personal Beliefs:** A person who harbors feelings of prejudice may become overly supportive of equality and diversity initiatives as a way to counteract their uncomfortable feelings.

Understanding these defense mechanisms in the context of everyday life helps us recognize the ways in which we and others cope with the complexities of life. Recognizing these patterns can lead to greater self-awareness, improved relationships, and healthier ways of managing stress and emotional challenges. It's important to note that while defense mechanisms can be protective and useful, overreliance on them can sometimes lead to unhealthy patterns of behavior.

5.4. Exercise: 10 MCQs with Answers at the End

Test your knowledge of defense mechanisms with these multiple-choice questions, designed to reinforce your understanding of their types and functions in everyday life. Answers are provided at the end for your reference.

1. **Repression is best described as:**

   A. Acting in the opposite way to one's unacceptable impulses.

   B. Shifting feelings to a more acceptable object.

C. Keeping distressing thoughts buried in the unconscious.

D. Offering plausible reasons for one's behavior.

2. **Which mechanism involves refusing to accept reality?**

A. Denial

B. Displacement

C. Sublimation

D. Regression

3. **Attributing one's own unacceptable feelings to others is known as:**

A. Projection

B. Rationalization

C. Repression

D. Reaction Formation

4. **Turning unacceptable urges into socially acceptable activities is called:**

A. Displacement

B. Sublimation

C. Regression

D. Denial

5. **What does rationalization involve?**

   A. Justifying behaviors with acceptable reasons

   B. Reverting to earlier behavior

   C. Transferring emotions to a substitute

   D. Ignoring painful realities

6. **Which mechanism is characterized by reverting to an earlier stage of development?**

   A. Projection

   B. Regression

   C. Rationalization

   D. Repression

7. **In defense mechanisms, displacement typically involves:**

   A. Altering one's impulses into constructive activities.

   B. Shifting feelings from the original source to a safer target.

   C. Denying the existence of a problem.

   D. Creating logical excuses for illogical behavior.

8. **Reaction formation is:**

   A. Transforming an unacceptable impulse into its opposite.

   B. Acting out unconscious desires in a socially acceptable way.

C. Shifting sexual or aggressive impulses to a less threatening target.

D. Completely blocking disturbing thoughts from consciousness.

9. A person who unconsciously feels incompetent may excessively brag about their abilities. This is an example of:

A. Sublimation

B. Projection

C. Reaction Formation

D. Denial

10. Intellectualization involves:

A. Focusing on the intellectual components of a situation to avoid emotional distress.

B. Redirecting feelings to a more acceptable object.

C. Behaving in a way opposite to one's true feelings.

D. Justifying one's actions with logical reasons.

Answers:

1. C. Keeping distressing thoughts buried in the unconscious.

2. A. Denial

3. A. Projection

4. B. Sublimation

5. A. Justifying behaviors with acceptable reasons

6. B. Regression

7. B. Shifting feelings from the original source to a safer target.

8. A. Transforming an unacceptable impulse into its opposite.

9. C. Reaction Formation

10. A. Focusing on the intellectual components of a situation to avoid emotional distress.

These questions are designed to deepen your understanding of defense mechanisms and how they function in various contexts, enhancing your ability to recognize and interpret these psychological strategies in daily life.

Chapter 6: The Therapeutic Process

6.1. Techniques in Psychoanalytic Therapy

Psychoanalytic therapy, rooted in the theories developed by Sigmund Freud, employs a range of techniques aimed at bringing the unconscious into conscious awareness. By doing so, it seeks to help individuals understand and resolve their deep-seated emotional issues and internal conflicts. Let's explore some of the key techniques used in this therapeutic approach.

1. **Free Association:** This foundational technique involves encouraging the patient to verbalize thoughts, including random or seemingly unimportant ones, without censorship or filtering. This process helps in uncovering hidden memories and emotions that are causing psychological distress.

2. **Dream Analysis:** As discussed earlier, Freud considered dreams to be the "royal road to the unconscious." In dream analysis, therapists help patients decode the symbolism in their dreams to reveal underlying thoughts and feelings.

3. **Interpretation:** This involves the therapist offering explanations about the unconscious motivations that could be driving the patient's behavior, thoughts, or feelings. It's a delicate process that requires the therapist to balance providing insight without overwhelming the patient.

4. **Transference:** This occurs when patients project feelings about important people in their lives onto the therapist. By analyzing and processing these transference reactions, patients can gain insight into their relationships and emotional patterns.

5. **Resistance:** During therapy, patients might show resistance to discussing certain topics or expressing certain emotions. Therapists work to help patients understand this resistance and its underlying causes, which often points to important areas of conflict within the patient's psyche.

6. **Use of Countertransference:** Countertransference refers to the therapist's emotional response to the patient. It can provide valuable insights into the patient's experiences and emotional state. Therapists must be aware of and manage their own responses to maintain effectiveness.

7. **Working Through:** This is the process of repeatedly going over and exploring the issues that arise in therapy. It helps patients understand the patterns in their thoughts and behaviors and learn how to change these patterns.

8. **Projective Testing:** While less common in contemporary psychoanalysis, techniques like the Rorschach inkblot test and the Thematic Apperception Test (TAT) were historically used to uncover unconscious desires, fears, and struggles.

Psychoanalytic therapy is a deep, often intensive process that goes beyond the symptoms to explore the intricate workings of the mind. Its techniques aim to bring clarity and understanding to the complexities of the human psyche, offering a path towards psychological healing and personal growth.

6.2. Transference and Countertransference

Transference and countertransference are two key concepts in psychoanalytic therapy that significantly influence the therapeutic relationship and the process of healing. Understanding these phenomena is crucial for both the therapist and the patient in navigating the complexities of therapy.

Transference:

1. **Definition:** Transference occurs when a patient unconsciously redirects feelings and desires, particularly those unresolved from childhood, onto the therapist. These feelings are usually associated with significant figures in the patient's past, like parents or caregivers.

2. **Manifestation:** It can manifest in various forms, such as idealization of the therapist, intense dependency, extreme anger, or even romantic feelings. For example, a patient might react to the therapist with the same anger and frustration they felt towards a parent.

3. **Therapeutic Role:** Transference provides a valuable window into the patient's inner world and relational dynamics. By exploring and interpreting these transference reactions, therapists can help patients understand their unresolved issues and work towards resolving them.

Countertransference:

1. **Definition:** Countertransference is the therapist's emotional reaction to the patient, often influenced by the therapist's own unconscious feelings and past experiences.

2. **Challenges and Benefits:** While countertransference can be challenging, as it might affect the therapist's objectivity, it can also be used therapeutically. A therapist's awareness and understanding of their own reactions can provide insights into the patient's emotional state and behaviors.

3. **Management:** Effective management of countertransference is crucial. Therapists often undergo their own psychoanalytic training and therapy to better understand and control these reactions.

The interplay of transference and countertransference is a dynamic and integral part of the psychoanalytic process. It requires careful navigation and skilled handling by the therapist. These phenomena not only enrich the therapeutic process but also facilitate deeper insight and understanding of the patient's emotional struggles and relational patterns. For the patient, working through transference can lead to significant breakthroughs in therapy, allowing for the resolution of longstanding psychological issues.

6.3. Efficacy and Criticism of Psychoanalytic Therapy

Psychoanalytic therapy, a cornerstone of Freudian psychology, has been both praised for its depth and criticized for various aspects. Understanding its efficacy and the criticisms it faces is essential for a balanced view of this therapeutic approach.

Efficacy of Psychoanalytic Therapy:

1. **Depth of Insight:** One of the strengths of psychoanalytic therapy is its focus on achieving deep and lasting insight into the patient's emotional issues and unconscious patterns. This can lead to significant changes in personality and behavior over time.

2. **Long-Term Benefits:** Patients who undergo successful psychoanalytic therapy often report long-term benefits, including improved relationships, better self-understanding, and resolution of deep-seated emotional issues.

3. **Treatment of Complex Issues:** It is particularly noted for its effectiveness in treating complex psychological conditions that other forms of therapy might not address as thoroughly, such as deep-rooted personality disorders or issues stemming from childhood trauma.

Criticisms of Psychoanalytic Therapy:

1. **Lack of Empirical Support:** One of the main criticisms is the lack of empirical evidence supporting its efficacy. Psychoanalytic concepts are often considered difficult to measure and quantify, which challenges its validity in the eyes of some in the scientific community.

2. **Time-Consuming and Costly:** Psychoanalytic therapy is often a long-term process, requiring years of sessions. This can make it time-consuming and expensive, limiting its accessibility to a broader range of patients.

3. **Overemphasis on Childhood and Sexuality:** Critics argue that psychoanalysis overemphasizes the role of childhood experiences and sexual conflicts in determining adult behavior and personality.

4. **Subjectivity and Interpretation:** The subjective nature of the therapy, particularly in the interpretation of dreams and transference, is another point of contention. Critics suggest that it can lead to therapist bias and misinterpretation.

5. **Cultural and Gender Bias:** Early psychoanalytic theories have been criticized for cultural and gender biases, particularly in the way they address female psychology and experiences.

Despite these criticisms, psychoanalytic therapy continues to be a significant and influential approach in psychology and psychotherapy. Its focus on the unconscious, the importance of early experiences, and the dynamics of the patient-therapist relationship have contributed profoundly to the understanding and treatment of psychological issues. However, like any therapeutic approach, it has its limitations and is continually evolving to address these criticisms and incorporate new insights and research findings.

6.4. Exercise: 10 MCQs with Answers at the End

Enhance your understanding of psychoanalytic therapy with these multiple-choice questions. These questions cover key concepts from Chapter 6, focusing on the techniques, efficacy, and criticisms of psychoanalytic therapy. Answers are provided at the end for your reference.

1. **Psychoanalytic therapy primarily aims to:**

   A. Change behavioral patterns through conditioning.

   B. Provide deep insight into unconscious motivations.

C. Offer immediate solutions to life problems.

D. Focus on cognitive restructuring.

2. In psychoanalytic therapy, free association involves:

A. The patient talking freely about whatever comes to mind.

B. The therapist interpreting the patient's dreams.

C. The patient remaining silent for long periods.

D. Guided imagery exercises.

3. Dream analysis in psychoanalysis is used to:

A. Predict future events based on dreams.

B. Understand the literal meanings of dreams.

C. Explore the unconscious meanings of dreams.

D. Improve the quality of sleep.

4. Transference in psychoanalytic therapy refers to:

A. The therapist's feelings towards the patient.

B. The patient's transfer of emotions to the therapist, related to other figures in their life.

C. Physical transfer of emotions.

D. The transfer of therapy techniques.

5. A major criticism of psychoanalytic therapy is its:

A. Lack of focus on the patient's past.

B. Overemphasis on empirical evidence.

C. Lengthy and costly nature.

D. Excessive use of medication.

6. **Countertransference is defined as:**

A. The patient's emotional reaction to therapy.

B. The therapist's unconscious emotional response to the patient.

C. Mutual emotional exchange between patient and therapist.

D. The therapist's deliberate use of emotion in therapy.

7. **Which technique involves the therapist explaining the meaning behind a patient's behavior or thoughts?**

A. Interpretation

B. Projection

C. Displacement

D. Rationalization

8. **One of the strengths of psychoanalytic therapy is its:**

A. Quick resolution of symptoms.

B. Focus on surface-level symptoms.

C. Ability to provide deep, long-term insight.

D. Use of medication to treat disorders.

9. **Which concept in psychoanalysis focuses on the patient's reluctance to discuss or engage with certain topics?**

A. Resistance

B. Regression

C. Repression

D. Rationalization

10. **The therapeutic process of working through in psychoanalysis involves:**

A. Rapidly changing therapy techniques.

B. Discussing the same issues repeatedly to gain deeper understanding.

C. Physical exercises to improve mental health.

D. Working through physical pain.

Answers:

1. B. Provide deep insight into unconscious motivations.

2. A. The patient talking freely about whatever comes to mind.

3. C. Explore the unconscious meanings of dreams.

4. B. The patient's transfer of emotions to the therapist, related to other figures in their life.

5. C. Lengthy and costly nature.

6. B. The therapist's unconscious emotional response to the patient.

7. A. Interpretation

8. C. Ability to provide deep, long-term insight.

9. A. Resistance

10. B. Discussing the same issues repeatedly to gain deeper understanding.

These questions are designed to deepen your understanding of psychoanalytic therapy, its techniques, and the critical discourse surrounding it, enhancing your knowledge of this influential psychological therapy approach.

Chapter 7: Freud's Influence on Culture

7.1. Freudian Concepts in Popular Culture

Sigmund Freud's impact extends far beyond the realm of psychology into the broader cultural landscape. His theories have permeated various aspects of popular culture, influencing literature, movies, art, and everyday language. Let's explore how Freudian concepts have become part of our cultural fabric.

1. **Everyday Language:** Freudian terminology like "Freudian slip" (a verbal mistake that is thought to reveal an unconscious belief, thought, or emotion), "ego," and "Oedipus complex" are commonly used in everyday language, often without awareness of their psychoanalytic origins.

2. **Film and Television:** Freud's theories have inspired countless movies and TV shows. Concepts like the unconscious, repression, and psychosexual development are frequently explored in plotlines, character developments, and themes. For example, Alfred Hitchcock's "Psycho" is heavily influenced by Freudian themes, particularly those of the Oedipus complex and psychosexual development.

3. **Literature:** Many writers have drawn on Freudian psychology to develop complex characters and narratives. From the subtle exploration of unconscious motivations in F. Scott Fitzgerald's "The Great Gatsby" to more explicit references in the works of authors like Virginia Woolf and James Joyce, Freudian concepts have significantly influenced literary analysis and criticism.

4. **Art and Artistic Expression:** Freud's exploration of the unconscious has had a profound impact on the art world, particularly in movements like Surrealism. Artists like Salvador Dalí and René Magritte created works that delved into the dreamlike realms of the unconscious mind, embodying Freud's ideas about dreams and the hidden depths of the psyche.

5. **Humor and Jokes:** Freud also explored the psychology of humor, suggesting that jokes and comedy offer a release from repression and provide insight into the unconscious. The use of Freudian concepts in humor is a testament to their pervasiveness in popular culture.

6. **Education and Critical Theory:** Freudian psychoanalysis has been integrated into various fields of study, including literary theory, feminist theory, film studies, and cultural studies. It provides a lens for analyzing the psychological underpinnings of cultural artifacts and societal trends.

Freud's influence on popular culture demonstrates the extensive reach of his theories. Whether in the arts, language, entertainment, or academia, Freudian concepts continue to offer a rich source of insight and inspiration, reflecting the enduring legacy of his work in understanding the complexities of the human mind and behavior.

7.2. Impact on Art and Literature

Freud's theories have had a profound impact on the worlds of art and literature, infusing these fields with a deeper exploration of the human psyche, unconscious motivations, and hidden desires. This influence has led to the creation of works that are not only aesthetically profound but also rich in psychological complexity.

Impact on Literature:

1. **Character Analysis:** Freud's insights into the human psyche revolutionized the way characters are analyzed in literature. Characters in novels and plays began to be examined not just for their actions but for the unconscious motivations driving those actions.

2. **Themes of Conflict:** Freud's emphasis on internal psychological conflict, particularly in his theory of psychosexual development, has influenced the themes of many literary works. Conflicts driven by repressed desires, familial relationships, and societal constraints became more prominently explored.

3. **Stream of Consciousness:** Techniques like stream of consciousness in literature, used effectively by writers like

Virginia Woolf and James Joyce, reflect Freud's influence. This narrative style delves into the continuous flow of a character's thoughts and feelings, mirroring Freud's emphasis on the unconscious.

4. **Psychoanalytic Literary Criticism:** This approach to literary criticism uses psychoanalytic theory as a lens to understand both the writer's psyche and the characters they create. It looks for symbols, themes, and conflicts that might represent unconscious material.

Impact on Art:

1. **Surrealism:** The Surrealist movement in art was heavily influenced by Freudian ideas. Artists like Salvador Dalí and René Magritte created dreamlike, bizarre scenes that aimed to reveal the workings of the unconscious mind.

2. **Symbolism:** Art began to incorporate more symbolic elements, often representing deeper psychological truths or conflicts. This was a direct reflection of Freud's belief in the symbolic nature of dreams and the unconscious.

3. **Exploration of Identity:** Artists influenced by Freudian psychology often explore themes of identity, self-perception, and the human condition, delving into the complexities and contradictions inherent in the psyche.

4. **Emotional Expressionism:** The movement towards expressing raw, unfiltered emotions in art can also be linked to Freud's focus on unearthing repressed feelings and emotions.

In both art and literature, Freud's theories opened new avenues for expression and interpretation, allowing artists and writers to explore the depths of human emotion, thought, and experience in innovative and profound ways. His influence has helped shape the way we understand and interact with artistic and literary works, adding a rich layer of psychological interpretation to the appreciation of culture and creativity.

7.3. Freud's Legacy in Contemporary Thought

Sigmund Freud's impact on contemporary thought extends far beyond the realm of psychoanalysis, influencing various fields and continuing to spark debate and discussion. While some of his ideas have been revised or critiqued, his overall contribution to our understanding of the mind and culture remains significant.

Psychology and Psychiatry:

1. **Unconscious Mind:** Freud's concept of the unconscious mind is one of his most enduring contributions. While the specifics of his theories are often debated, the idea that much of our mental life is unconscious is widely accepted.

2. **Psychotherapy:** Freud's development of psychotherapy laid the groundwork for various therapeutic approaches. Concepts such as transference and the therapeutic alliance are still central in many forms of therapy.

3. **Child Development:** Freud's emphasis on early childhood experiences as determinants of adult personality has influenced contemporary views on child development, despite some of his specific theories being critiqued.

Cultural and Social Sciences:

1. **Critical Theory:** Freud's theories have been instrumental in the development of critical theory, particularly in fields like literature, film, and gender studies. His ideas have been used to explore the psychological underpinnings of cultural and social phenomena.

2. **Gender and Sexuality Studies:** Freud's exploration of sexuality, though controversial, opened discussions on sexual identity and psychology. His work influenced later theorists like Judith Butler and Jacques Lacan, who expanded on or contested his views.

3. **Popular Culture:** Freud's concepts continue to permeate popular culture, influencing how we understand and talk about our motivations, fears, and desires.

Criticism and Revision:

1. **Scientific Scrutiny:** Some of Freud's theories have been criticized for lacking empirical support. In response, contemporary psychoanalysis often incorporates more evidence-based approaches.

2. **Cultural Context:** Critics argue that Freud's theories were a product of their time and cultural context, and may not be universally applicable. This has led to a more culturally sensitive approach in modern psychoanalytic practice.

3. **Revised Theories:** Many of Freud's ideas have been revised or expanded upon by later theorists, integrating new research findings from fields like neuroscience and developmental psychology.

Freud's legacy in contemporary thought is complex and multifaceted. While some aspects of his work have been critiqued and revised, his fundamental contributions to our understanding of the human mind, behavior, and culture remain influential. His ability to provoke thought and inspire further inquiry is perhaps one of the most significant aspects of his enduring legacy.

7.4. Exercise: 10 MCQs with Answers at the End

Test your knowledge on the influence of Freud's theories in contemporary culture and thought with these multiple-choice questions. This exercise covers various aspects of Freud's legacy as explored in Chapter 7. Answers are provided at the end for your reference.

1. **Freud's concept of the unconscious mind has primarily influenced:**

A. Neuroscience

B. Quantum physics

C. Modern psychotherapy

D. Economics

2. **Which artistic movement was heavily influenced by Freud's theories?**

A. Impressionism

B. Surrealism

C. Cubism

D. Abstract Expressionism

3. **Freud's theories have been instrumental in the development of:**

A. Classical physics

B. Critical theory

C. Algebra

D. Computer science

4. **In literature, Freud's impact can be seen in:**

A. Increased focus on external landscapes

B. The use of stream of consciousness technique

C. Emphasis on science fiction themes

D. The decline of the novel

5. **Freud's ideas about early childhood experiences predominantly influenced:**

A. Astrophysics

B. Child development theories

C. Political science

D. Linguistics

6. **Which field utilizes Freud's theories to explore the psychological underpinnings of cultural phenomena?**

A. Environmental science

B. Gender and sexuality studies

C. Mechanical engineering

D. Urban planning

7. **In popular culture, a 'Freudian slip' is understood as:**

A. A fashion trend

B. A verbal mistake revealing an unconscious thought

C. A type of dance move

D. A recipe in cooking

8. **The concept of transference, introduced by Freud, is especially important in:**

A. Economics

B. Theoretical physics

C. Psychotherapy

D. Culinary arts

9. **Freud's exploration of sexuality led to discussions and developments in:**

A. Space exploration

B. Sexual identity and psychology

C. Organic chemistry

D. Paleontology

10. **One of the criticisms of Freud's theories in the modern context is their:**

A. Overemphasis on empirical evidence

B. Lack of scientific scrutiny

C. Focus on technological advancements

D. Emphasis on environmental factors

Answers:

1. C. Modern psychotherapy

2. B. Surrealism

3. B. Critical theory

4. B. The use of stream of consciousness technique

5. B. Child development theories

6. B. Gender and sexuality studies

7. B. A verbal mistake revealing an unconscious thought

8. C. Psychotherapy

9. B. Sexual identity and psychology

10. B. Lack of scientific scrutiny

These questions are designed to help you reflect on the extensive influence of Freudian concepts across various fields and their presence in everyday language and culture. They also touch upon the criticisms and adaptations of Freud's theories in the modern era.

Chapter 8: The Oedipus Complex

8.1. Origins and Explanation of the Oedipus Complex

One of Freud's most famous and controversial theories is the Oedipus complex, a central concept in Freudian psychology that explains the dynamics of the psyche in early childhood.

Origins of the Concept:

1. **Name Derivation:** The term "Oedipus complex" is derived from the Greek myth of Oedipus, who unknowingly killed his father and married his mother. Freud used this story to illustrate his theory of unconscious desires in children.

2. **Development of the Theory:** Freud developed the concept of the Oedipus complex as part of his broader theory of psychosexual development. He proposed that this complex occurs during the phallic stage of development, which typically happens around the ages of three to six years.

Explanation of the Oedipus Complex:

1. In Boys (Oedipus Complex):

  - Boys develop an unconscious sexual attraction towards their mother and a simultaneous jealousy and rivalry with their father, whom they view as a competitor for the mother's affection.

  - Freud believed that boys fear retaliation from their fathers (castration anxiety) and eventually identify with the father, adopting his characteristics and values, as a way to resolve the conflict.

2. In Girls (Electra Complex):

  - The counterpart in girls is known as the Electra complex, named after another Greek mythological figure.

  - Freud theorized that girls initially attach sexually to their mothers, but upon realizing they do not have a penis, they shift their attachment to their fathers, developing penis envy. This leads to a rivalry with the mother and a desire for the father's affection.

3. Resolution of the Complex:

  - The resolution of the Oedipus complex is crucial in Freud's theory for healthy psychosexual development. Through identification with the same-sex parent, children internalize norms, values, and roles appropriate to their gender.

4. Significance in Psychoanalytic Theory:

- The Oedipus complex is central to Freud's understanding of the formation of the superego, the development of gender identity, and the origins of neurosis in later life.

The concept of the Oedipus complex has been subject to much debate and criticism over the years, particularly regarding its universality and interpretation of female psychosexual development. However, it remains a foundational element in Freudian psychoanalytic theory and continues to influence psychoanalytic thought and practice.

8.2. Implications and Criticisms

The Oedipus complex, as proposed by Freud, has far-reaching implications in psychoanalytic theory and has also been the subject of significant criticism and debate.

Implications of the Oedipus Complex:

1. **Personality Development:** Freud believed that the successful resolution of the Oedipus complex was key to developing a healthy adult personality. Unresolved Oedipal conflicts were thought to lead to neuroses and problematic adult behaviors.

2. **Gender and Sexual Identity:** The Oedipus complex is central to Freud's theory of how children form their gender and sexual identities, suggesting that identification with the same-sex parent is crucial in this process.

3. **Formation of the Superego:** The resolution of the Oedipus complex leads to the development of the superego, according to Freud. The child internalizes the morals and values of the same-sex parent, which become the basis for their conscience.

4. **Influence on Relationships:** Freud theorized that unresolved Oedipal conflicts could influence an individual's future romantic relationships, potentially leading to partner choices that reflect unresolved childhood dynamics.

Criticisms of the Oedipus Complex:

1. **Lack of Empirical Evidence:** One of the primary criticisms is the lack of solid empirical evidence supporting the Oedipus complex. Critics argue that it is based more on Freud's interpretations than on observable, scientific data.

2. **Cultural Bias and Universality:** Critics have pointed out that Freud's theories, including the Oedipus complex, may reflect Western, patriarchal biases of his time. The assumption that the Oedipus complex is a universal phenomenon has been questioned by cross-cultural studies.

3. **Views on Female Development:** The concept of the Electra complex (the female counterpart to the Oedipus complex) and the notion of "penis envy" have been particularly criticized for being misogynistic and for offering a male-centric view of female psychosexual development.

4. **Modern Psychoanalytic Views:** Contemporary psychoanalysts and psychologists have revised or moved away from the classic interpretation of the Oedipus complex. Many now view the complex in terms of more nuanced emotional conflicts and identifications during early development.

Despite these criticisms, the Oedipus complex remains a significant and historically influential concept in psychoanalysis. It has spurred extensive discussion and exploration in areas of psychology, sexuality, gender studies, and cultural theory, reflecting the lasting impact of Freud's ideas on understanding human behavior and development.

8.3. Oedipus Complex in Modern Psychoanalysis

The Oedipus complex, a foundational concept in Freudian psychoanalysis, has undergone significant reinterpretation and adaptation in modern psychoanalytic thought. While the basic premise of the complex remains influential, contemporary psychoanalysts have expanded and nuanced its interpretation.

Reinterpretations and Adaptations:

1. **Broader Emotional Conflicts:** Modern psychoanalysts often interpret the Oedipus complex in terms of broader emotional and relational dynamics rather than strictly sexual desires. This includes the child's evolving understanding of and navigation through family relationships, power dynamics, and emotional attachments.

2. **Gender and Sexuality:** Contemporary psychoanalysis has moved away from the traditional gendered views of the Oedipus and Electra complexes. Modern theorists focus more on the development of gender and sexual identities as complex processes influenced by a variety of factors beyond the family dynamics described by Freud.

3. **Cultural Context and Diversity:** Modern psychoanalysis considers cultural and societal influences on the development of children more thoroughly. This approach acknowledges that the dynamics described in the Oedipus complex can vary significantly across different cultural and social contexts.

4. **Parent-Child Relationship Dynamics:** The focus has shifted to a more nuanced understanding of parent-child relationships. This includes exploring how children identify with parents and other caregivers, and how these relationships impact their emotional and psychological development.

5. **Symbolic Interpretation:** The Oedipus complex is sometimes viewed more symbolically, representing the child's journey of

individuation and separation from the parents, rather than literally as Freud initially proposed.

6. **Influence on Therapy:** In therapeutic settings, insights derived from the Oedipus complex are used to explore and understand a patient's childhood experiences and their impact on adult life, particularly in terms of relationships and emotional patterns.

Contemporary Critiques and Debates:

Modern psychoanalysis continues to debate and critique the concept of the Oedipus complex. Some practitioners view it as an essential tool for understanding psychological development, while others believe it needs further revision or question its relevance in contemporary practice.

Overall, the Oedipus complex in modern psychoanalysis serves as a bridge connecting Freud's foundational ideas with contemporary understanding of human development. It remains a significant concept, albeit one that is continually evolving to encompass a more diverse and complex understanding of human psychology.

8.4. Exercise: 10 MCQs with Answers at the End

Test your understanding of the Oedipus complex and its role in modern psychoanalysis with these multiple-choice questions. This exercise will help reinforce your knowledge of the concepts discussed in Chapter 8. Answers are provided at the end for your reference.

1. **The Oedipus complex primarily occurs during which stage of psychosexual development?**

   A. Oral

   B. Anal

   C. Phallic

   D. Latency

2. **According to Freud, the resolution of the Oedipus complex leads to the development of:**

   A. The id

   B. The ego

   C. The superego

   D. The unconscious

3. **In the context of the Oedipus complex, castration anxiety is experienced by:**

A. Girls in the Electra complex

B. Boys in the Oedipus complex

C. Both boys and girls in the phallic stage

D. Parents of the child

4. **Which concept is considered the female counterpart to the Oedipus complex in Freudian theory?**

A. Penis envy

B. The Electra complex

C. Maternal instinct

D. Paternal fixation

5. **Modern psychoanalysis tends to view the Oedipus complex in terms of:**

A. Strictly sexual desires

B. Broader emotional and relational dynamics

C. Only biological impulses

D. Literal interpretations of childhood memories

6. **Freud believed that unresolved Oedipal conflicts could lead to:**

   A. Improved cognitive abilities

   B. Neuroses and problematic behaviors in adulthood

   C. Enhanced creativity

   D. Better physical health

7. **Contemporary critiques of the Oedipus complex often focus on its:**

   A. Overemphasis on empirical evidence

   B. Lack of consideration for cultural and societal influences

   C. Focus on modern technological impacts

   D. Emphasis on physical health

8. **In therapy, insights from the Oedipus complex are used to explore:**

   A. Only past sexual desires

   B. Childhood experiences and their impact on adult life

   C. Future career aspirations

   D. Physical ailments

9. **The Electra complex in Freudian theory involves a girl's:**

   A. Attachment and hostility toward the mother

   B. Desire to emulate the father

   C. Fear of losing the mother's love

   D. Identification with the father

10. **Which stage follows the resolution of the Oedipus complex in Freud's theory?**

   A. Oral

   B. Anal

   C. Phallic

   D. Latency

Answers:

1. C. Phallic

2. C. The superego

3. B. Boys in the Oedipus complex

4. B. The Electra complex

5. B. Broader emotional and relational dynamics

6. B. Neuroses and problematic behaviors in adulthood

7. B. Lack of consideration for cultural and societal influences

8. B. Childhood experiences and their impact on adult life

9. D. Identification with the father

10. D. Latency

These questions are designed to enhance your understanding of the Oedipus complex, its implications, criticisms, and how it is viewed and utilized in modern psychoanalysis. Reflecting on these questions can deepen your comprehension of this complex and controversial aspect of Freudian theory.

Chapter 9: Anxiety and Ego Defense

9.1. Freud's Theory of Anxiety

Sigmund Freud's exploration of anxiety is a pivotal aspect of his psychoanalytic theory, providing insight into how anxiety functions within the psyche and its role in human behavior.

Basic Tenets of Freud's Theory of Anxiety:

1. **Source of Anxiety:** Freud postulated that anxiety stems from unconscious conflicts that arise when the ego perceives a threat from the external world, the id's desires, or the superego's moral constraints. This perceived threat leads to a state of unease or tension, which we experience as anxiety.

2. **Types of Anxiety According to Freud:**

   - **Reality Anxiety:** This is the fear of real-world events, akin to fear. For example, being anxious about a dangerous situation.

   - **Neurotic Anxiety:** This arises from a fear that the instincts of the id will take control and cause one to do something for which one will be punished.

- **Moral Anxiety:** Stemming from the superego, this type of anxiety is a fear of violating moral or societal codes, leading to feelings of guilt or shame.

3. **Role of the Ego:** In Freud's view, the ego plays a crucial role in managing these types of anxieties. It uses various defense mechanisms to protect the individual from experiencing anxiety directly.

4. **Signal Theory of Anxiety:** Freud also proposed that anxiety serves as a signal to the ego that something is amiss and requires attention. This signal function of anxiety can lead to either adaptive or maladaptive responses.

Implications of Freud's Theory of Anxiety:

1. **Understanding Mental Disorders:** Freud's theory laid the groundwork for understanding various mental disorders in terms of anxiety. For instance, phobias, obsessions, and compulsions were seen as manifestations of underlying anxiety.

2. **Development of Psychotherapy:** This theory contributed to the development of techniques in psychotherapy aimed at uncovering the unconscious conflicts causing anxiety and helping patients find healthier ways to cope.

3. **Influence on Later Theories:** Freud's ideas about anxiety influenced subsequent theorists and psychologists, who expanded upon or modified his concepts, integrating them with new research and perspectives in psychology.

Freud's theory of anxiety is a cornerstone of his psychoanalytic theory, offering a framework for understanding the complexities of human emotions and behavior. While modern psychology has developed new approaches to understanding and treating anxiety, Freud's contributions remain influential in the field.

9.2. The Role of Ego in Managing Anxiety

In Freudian psychology, the ego plays a central role in managing anxiety. It acts as a mediator between the id, the superego, and the external world, employing various strategies to balance these often conflicting demands and protect the individual from anxiety. Let's delve into how the ego functions in this capacity.

Mechanisms of Anxiety Management by the Ego:

1. **Defense Mechanisms:** The primary way the ego manages anxiety is through defense mechanisms. These are unconscious psychological strategies that reduce the anxiety arising from unacceptable or harmful stimuli. Defense mechanisms include repression, denial, projection, rationalization, displacement, sublimation, and others.

2. **Reality Testing:** The ego engages in reality testing to assess whether the anxiety-provoking situation is based in reality or if it is a product of internal fears or fantasies. This helps in distinguishing between realistic fears and neurotic anxieties.

3. **Problem-Solving:** When faced with a realistic source of anxiety, the ego employs problem-solving strategies to deal with the situation effectively. This can involve planning, seeking help, or taking direct action to mitigate the source of anxiety.

4. **Regulating Id Impulses:** The ego must balance the desires of the id, which can be a source of anxiety when they conflict with societal norms or personal morals. The ego restrains these impulses and finds acceptable ways of expressing them.

5. **Mediating Superego Demands:** The ego also has to manage the demands of the superego, which can cause moral anxiety. It navigates these demands by finding compromises that satisfy moral standards without causing too much distress.

Adaptive vs. Maladaptive Responses:

1. **Adaptive Strategies:** Healthy ego functioning leads to adaptive strategies for managing anxiety, such as problem-solving, using humor, or sublimation. These responses help in effectively addressing the source of anxiety without causing additional psychological distress.

2. **Maladaptive Strategies:** Overreliance on certain defense mechanisms, like denial or projection, can be maladaptive. They may provide short-term relief from anxiety but can lead to dysfunctional behavior patterns and hinder emotional growth and resolution of underlying issues.

The role of the ego in managing anxiety is a fundamental aspect of Freudian psychology and psychoanalytic therapy. Understanding how the ego operates to balance internal and external demands provides crucial insight into human behavior and the development of various psychological disorders. This understanding also guides therapeutic interventions aimed at strengthening ego functions and promoting healthier ways of dealing with anxiety.

9.3. Case Studies of Anxiety and Defense

Exploring case studies in the context of Freudian psychology provides valuable insights into how anxiety manifests and is managed through various defense mechanisms. These case studies illuminate the intricate interplay between unconscious conflicts, anxiety, and ego defenses in real-life scenarios.

Case Study 1: Phobia in a Child (Little Hans)

One of Freud's famous case studies involved a five-year-old boy known as Little Hans, who developed a phobia of horses. Freud interpreted this phobia as a manifestation of the Oedipus complex. The fear of horses represented Hans' castration anxiety, with the horse being a symbolic stand-in for his father, a figure both feared and admired. Hans' anxiety and phobia were seen as defenses against his unconscious fears and desires related to his father.

Case Study 2: Obsessive-Compulsive Disorder

Another case involved an adult with obsessive-compulsive disorder (OCD). The individual exhibited compulsive hand-washing and ritualistic behaviors. Freud interpreted these compulsions as defenses against unconscious thoughts and impulses that were anxiety-provoking. The act of washing hands was seen as a symbolic attempt to cleanse oneself of these forbidden thoughts.

Case Study 3: Hysteria (Anna O.)

Anna O., a patient of Freud's colleague Josef Breuer, suffered from hysteria, characterized by physical symptoms like paralysis and disturbances in vision, without any apparent organic cause. Freud and Breuer proposed that these symptoms were manifestations of repressed traumatic experiences and unresolved emotional conflicts. The physical symptoms served as defenses against the anxiety stemming from these repressed memories.

Insights from Case Studies:

1. **Representation of Internal Conflicts:** These cases illustrate how external symptoms, fears, and behaviors can be representations of deep internal conflicts and anxieties.

2. **Defense Mechanisms at Work:** The case studies demonstrate the role of defense mechanisms in managing anxiety. Phobias, compulsions, and physical symptoms can be seen as ways the ego attempts to cope with and mitigate anxiety arising from unconscious conflicts.

3. **Therapeutic Implications:** Understanding the underlying anxieties and defense mechanisms can guide therapeutic interventions. In these cases, bringing the unconscious conflicts into conscious awareness was key to alleviating the symptoms.

4. **Complexity of Human Psyche:** These case studies underscore the complexity of the human psyche and the intricate ways in which psychological disorders can manifest, driven by the dynamics between the id, ego, and superego.

While the interpretations in these case studies are specific to Freudian psychoanalysis and have been subject to criticism and debate, they continue to provide valuable frameworks for understanding the relationship between anxiety, unconscious conflicts, and defense mechanisms in psychology.

9.4. Exercise: 10 MCQs with Answers at the End

Test your knowledge of Freud's theory of anxiety and the role of ego in managing anxiety with these multiple-choice questions.

This exercise covers the key concepts discussed in Chapter 9. Answers are provided at the end for your reference.

1. **According to Freud, anxiety primarily arises from:**

   A. External threats

   B. Conflicts between the id, ego, and superego

   C. Lack of sleep

   D. Poor diet

2. **Neurotic anxiety in Freud's theory is the fear of:**

   A. Loss of loved ones

   B. Natural disasters

   C. Instincts of the id taking control

   D. Violating moral codes

3. **The defense mechanism of displacement involves:**

   A. Redirecting emotions to a substitute target

   B. Transforming unacceptable urges into socially acceptable activities

   C. Denying the reality of a situation

   D. Reverting to an earlier stage of development

4. **Reality testing in managing anxiety is used by the ego to:**

A. Assess whether an anxiety-provoking situation is based in reality

B. Ignore real-world events

C. Increase the level of anxiety

D. Focus on unconscious desires

5. **An example of moral anxiety is:**

A. Fear of a dangerous animal

B. Guilt over violating one's moral standards

C. Anxiety about social situations

D. Worry about failing a test

6. **Freud's concept of signal theory of anxiety suggests that anxiety:**

A. Has no real purpose

B. Is always harmful and debilitating

C. Serves as a warning to the ego that something is wrong

D. Is solely a product of the external environment

7. **In Freudian theory, a phobia is viewed as:**

A. A realistic fear of a specific object or situation

B. A manifestation of deeper, unconscious fears

C. Only a childhood phenomenon

D. Always linked to a traumatic event

8. **The ego uses defense mechanisms to:**

A. Increase anxiety levels

B. Balance the needs of the id and the superego

C. Weaken the superego

D. Enhance conscious awareness

9. **Which of the following is a defense mechanism?**

A. Rationalization

B. Intelligence

C. Memory loss

D. Physical exercise

10. **In psychoanalytic therapy, understanding a patient's anxiety can help in:**

A. Ignoring their unconscious conflicts

B. Prescribing medication

C. Exploring underlying psychological issues

D. Focusing solely on their physical symptoms

Answers:

1. B. Conflicts between the id, ego, and superego

2. C. Instincts of the id taking control

3. A. Redirecting emotions to a substitute target

4. A. Assess whether an anxiety-provoking situation is based in reality

5. B. Guilt over violating one's moral standards

6. C. Serves as a warning to the ego that something is wrong

7. B. A manifestation of deeper, unconscious fears

8. B. Balance the needs of the id and the superego

9. A. Rationalization

10. C. Exploring underlying psychological issues

These questions are designed to enhance your understanding of Freud's views on anxiety, the role of the ego in managing it, and the significance of these concepts in psychoanalytic therapy. Reflecting on these questions can deepen your comprehension of the complex relationship between anxiety, defense mechanisms, and the human psyche.

Chapter 10: The Role of Sexuality

10.1. Sexuality in Freudian Theory

Sigmund Freud's theories placed significant emphasis on sexuality, which he considered a driving force in human psychology and behavior. His views on sexuality were groundbreaking at the time and continue to be influential, albeit controversial.

Foundational Aspects of Sexuality in Freudian Theory:

1. **Libido:** Freud introduced the concept of libido, which he defined as the energy of the sexual drive. In his view, libido was a primary motivating force behind human behavior and psychological development.

2. **Psychosexual Development:** Freud proposed that sexual development occurs in stages, each characterized by the erogenous zone that is the source of the libido's gratification. These stages are oral, anal, phallic, latency, and genital. He believed that experiences during these stages significantly influence one's adult personality and sexual behavior.

3. **Oedipus Complex:** The Oedipus complex, which emerges during the phallic stage, is fundamentally linked to Freud's theory of sexuality. It involves the child's unconscious sexual desire for the opposite-sex parent and jealousy towards the same-sex parent.

4. **Infantile Sexuality:** Freud controversially suggested that sexuality is present even in infants and children, manifesting in behaviors related to different erogenous zones at various developmental stages.

5. **Repression and Sublimation:** Sexual desires that are deemed unacceptable or are repressed, according to Freud, can lead to psychological conflicts and neuroses. Sublimation, a defense mechanism, involves channeling these repressed sexual energies into socially acceptable activities.

Controversies and Criticisms:

1. **Overemphasis on Sexuality:** Freud has been criticized for overemphasizing the role of sexuality in psychological development and human motivation.

2. **Views on Female Sexuality:** Freud's views on female sexuality, particularly the concept of "penis envy," have been heavily criticized for being misogynistic and based on a male-centric perspective.

3. **Cultural and Historical Context:** Some critics argue that Freud's theories on sexuality reflect the Victorian era's attitudes and may not be applicable in different cultural or modern contexts.

4. **Impact on Psychotherapy:** Despite the controversies, Freud's focus on sexuality opened discussions on sexual health and psychology, leading to more openness in addressing sexual issues in psychotherapy.

Freud's theories on sexuality, while groundbreaking, are a product of their time and have been extensively debated and reevaluated. They have, however, undeniably influenced the field of psychology and the way sexuality is perceived in psychotherapy and broader society.

10.2. Development of Sexual Identity

Freud's theories on the development of sexual identity have had a profound impact on both psychology and the broader understanding of human sexuality. While his ideas have evolved and been critiqued over time, they laid important groundwork in the field.

Freudian Perspectives on Sexual Identity Development:

1. **Early Childhood Influences:** Freud believed that sexual identity begins to form in early childhood during the psychosexual stages. He theorized that the experiences and relationships a child has during these stages play a significant role in shaping their adult sexual identity.

2. **Oedipus and Electra Complexes:** Central to Freud's theory is the idea that the resolution of the Oedipus complex (in boys) and the Electra complex (in girls) during the phallic stage is crucial for healthy sexual identity development. The identification with the same-sex parent was seen as a key aspect of this process.

3. **Role of Identification and Imitation:** Freud posited that children develop their sexual identity by identifying with and imitating the same-sex parent. This identification process was thought to be how children internalize the sexual roles and behaviors deemed appropriate for their gender.

4. **The Concept of Bisexuality:** Freud also suggested that all individuals are inherently bisexual in their early stages of development, meaning they have the potential for both heterosexual and homosexual orientations. How they develop into one identity over the other was seen as a result of their psychosexual development and familial dynamics.

Modern Perspectives and Critiques:

1. **Broader Factors:** Contemporary psychology recognizes that the development of sexual identity is influenced by a broader range of factors, including biological, social, cultural, and environmental influences, not just family dynamics.

2. **Debate over Oedipal and Electra Complexes:** The concepts of the Oedipus and Electra complexes are viewed with skepticism by many modern psychologists, who argue that these theories are overly simplistic and not empirically supported.

3. **Diversity in Sexual Identity:** Modern understandings of sexual identity acknowledge a greater diversity and fluidity than Freud's binary approach. The role of individual experiences, societal influences, and biological factors are considered more prominently in current theories.

4. **Gender and Cultural Sensitivity:** There is a greater emphasis on understanding sexual identity development in a way that is sensitive to gender diversity and cultural differences, moving away from the rigid gender norms implicit in Freud's work.

The development of sexual identity is a complex and multifaceted process. While Freud's theories provided initial insights, contemporary psychology has expanded and revised these ideas to encompass a more inclusive and nuanced understanding of human sexuality.

10.3. Critiques of Freud's Views on Sexuality

Freud's theories on sexuality, groundbreaking in their time, have been subject to substantial critique and reassessment in modern psychological discourse. These critiques have focused on various aspects of his work, reflecting shifts in scientific understanding and societal attitudes towards sexuality.

Key Critiques of Freud's Views on Sexuality:

1. **Overemphasis on Sexuality:** Freud has been criticized for attributing too much importance to sexual drives in the development and functioning of personality. Critics argue that other factors, such as social, cultural, and environmental influences, play a significant role in human psychology.

2. **Biological Determinism:** Freud's theories are often seen as biologically deterministic, suggesting that human behavior and personality are largely driven by innate sexual instincts. This view is considered overly reductionist by many contemporary psychologists.

3. **Misogynistic Views:** Freud's theories, particularly concerning female sexuality and the concept of "penis envy," have been criticized for being misogynistic. Critics argue that these theories reflect the patriarchal biases of his time and fail to adequately or accurately represent female psychological development.

4. **Heteronormativity and Homophobia:** Freud's ideas about the development of sexual identity have been critiqued for perpetuating heteronormative views and pathologizing homosexuality. Modern psychology recognizes a greater diversity in sexual orientations and identities.

5. **Lack of Empirical Evidence:** Many of Freud's concepts, including his theories of sexuality, lack empirical support and are often based on case studies with limited generalizability. This has led to questions about the scientific validity of his theories.

6. **Cultural and Historical Context:** Critics point out that Freud's views on sexuality were heavily influenced by the cultural and historical context of his time, which may limit their applicability to modern society and diverse cultures.

7. **Alternative Theories:** Subsequent research and theories in psychology have provided alternative explanations for many of the phenomena Freud attributed to sexual drives, such as attachment theory's explanations for emotional bonds and behaviors.

Despite these critiques, Freud's work on sexuality remains a foundational element of psychoanalytic theory and has significantly influenced the discourse on human sexuality in various fields, including psychology, sociology, and gender studies. His theories sparked broader discussions and debates, leading to more nuanced and comprehensive understandings of human sexuality in contemporary thought.

10.4. Exercise: 10 MCQs with Answers at the End

Enhance your understanding of Freud's views on sexuality and the critiques of these views with these multiple-choice questions. This exercise covers the concepts discussed in Chapter 10. Answers are provided at the end for your reference.

1. **Freud's concept of libido primarily refers to:**

   A. General life energy

   B. The energy of the sexual drive

   C. Conscious thought processes

   D. Physical strength

2. **According to Freud, which stage is not part of psychosexual development?**

   A. Oral

   B. Anal

   C. Phallic

   D. Cognitive

3. **What does 'penis envy' in Freudian theory refer to?**

   A. A man's desire to be more masculine

   B. A woman's supposed jealousy of men

   C. A child's curiosity about gender differences

   D. A general envy of power and status

4. **A major criticism of Freud's theories on sexuality is their:**

   A. Emphasis on cultural factors

   B. Overemphasis on sexual factors

   C. Ignoring of childhood experiences

   D. Focus on empirical evidence

5. **Freud's concept of the Oedipus complex is related to:**

   A. The development of cognitive abilities

   B. The establishment of social norms

   C. The formation of sexual identity

   D. The onset of moral reasoning

6. **Freud's view on female sexuality has been criticized for being:**

   A. Empirically well-supported

   B. Inclusive of diverse sexual orientations

   C. Misogynistic and male-centric

D. Focused on gender equality

7. Freud's theory of sexuality suggests that sexual identity is formed during:

A. Early adulthood

B. Adolescence

C. Early childhood

D. Infancy

8. One of the critiques of Freud's sexual theories is their:

A. Avoidance of discussing infantile sexuality

B. Heteronormativity and pathologizing of homosexuality

C. Emphasis on environmental influences

D. Focus on non-sexual psychological factors

9. In Freudian theory, the resolution of the Oedipus complex leads to:

A. Decreased sexual interest

B. Development of the superego

C. Development of neuroses

D. Elimination of the id

10. **Which approach has provided alternative explanations to Freud's theories of sexual development?**

A. Quantum mechanics

B. Attachment theory

C. String theory

D. Classical physics

Answers:

1. B. The energy of the sexual drive

2. D. Cognitive

3. B. A woman's supposed jealousy of men

4. B. Overemphasis on sexual factors

5. C. The formation of sexual identity

6. C. Misogynistic and male-centric

7. C. Early childhood

8. B. Heteronormativity and pathologizing of homosexuality

9. B. Development of the superego

10. B. Attachment theory

These questions are designed to reinforce your understanding of Freud's theories on sexuality, their implications, and the criticisms they have faced, enhancing your comprehension of this significant aspect of Freudian theory. Reflecting on these questions can deepen your knowledge of the complexities and controversies surrounding Freud's views on human sexuality.

Chapter 11: Religion and Civilization

11.1. Freud's Views on Religion

Sigmund Freud's views on religion were complex and often controversial. He approached religion from a psychoanalytic perspective, analyzing it as a phenomenon rooted in the human psyche.

Key Aspects of Freud's Views on Religion:

1. **Religion as an Illusion:** Freud considered religion to be an illusion, a creation of the human mind to fulfill emotional and psychological needs. He argued that religious beliefs are the product of human wishes and desires, particularly the desire for security and protection.

2. **Oedipal Complex and Religion:** Freud connected the origins of religious belief to the Oedipus complex. He theorized that the universal image of a powerful, father-like God is a projection of the child's feelings towards their own father, representing a longing for a paternal figure who can alleviate the anxieties and vulnerabilities of life.

3. **Psychological Comfort and Control:** According to Freud, religion serves as a means of psychological comfort and control, offering answers to existential questions that cause anxiety, such as the fear of death and the unknown. It provides a sense of order and meaning in a world that can often feel chaotic and unpredictable.

4. **Collective Neurosis:** Freud controversially described religion as a "universal obsessional neurosis." He believed that religious rituals and beliefs are akin to the compulsive behaviors seen in individuals with neurosis, but on a collective scale.

5. **Critique of Religious Morality:** Freud also critiqued the moral aspects of religion, arguing that while religious teachings often promote ethical behavior, they can also lead to guilt, repression, and internal conflict.

Modern Interpretations and Critiques:

1. **Cultural and Historical Context:** Modern scholars note that Freud's views on religion were influenced by the cultural and historical context of his time. His critiques are often seen as reflecting the secular, scientific mindset of early 20th-century Europe.

2. **Psychological Need for Religion:** While Freud's view of religion as an illusion has been debated, his insights into the psychological needs that religion fulfills remain influential in the study of psychology and religion.

3. **Diversity of Religious Experience:** Contemporary thinkers often argue that Freud's analysis does not account for the diversity and complexity of religious experiences across different cultures and individuals.

4. **Integration with Other Theories:** Some modern psychoanalysts and psychologists have sought to integrate Freud's theories with more nuanced understandings of spirituality and religion, acknowledging the potential positive psychological impacts of religious beliefs and practices.

Freud's analysis of religion provides a unique perspective on the intersection between psychology and spirituality, offering a lens through which to explore the deeper emotional and psychological reasons behind religious beliefs and behaviors.

11.2. The Psychological Basis of Civilization

Freud's exploration of the psychological underpinnings of civilization is another significant aspect of his work, where he delves into how human psychological drives shape and are shaped by societal structures.

Key Concepts in Freud's Analysis of Civilization:

1. **Civilization as a Regulation of Desires:** Freud viewed civilization as a necessary system to regulate human desires and impulses, particularly aggressive and sexual drives. He believed that for civilization to function, these basic drives must be repressed or sublimated into socially acceptable forms.

2. **Conflict Between Individual and Society:** A central theme in Freud's view is the inherent conflict between the individual's quest for freedom (to satisfy instinctual desires) and the demands of civilization for order and conformity. This tension, he argued, is a source of much human discontent and psychological conflict.

3. **The Role of Superego in Society:** Freud saw the superego as not just an individual psychic entity but also as a cultural one. He suggested that the superego, with its internalized norms and morals, represents the influence of society on the individual. It's a mechanism through which societal rules become part of the individual psyche.

4. **Civilization and Neurosis:** Freud proposed that the repression required by civilization leads to the development of neurosis. He argued that the more advanced a civilization, the more widespread the neurosis among its people, as the demands for repression are greater.

5. **"Civilization and Its Discontents":** In his seminal work, Freud explored how the restrictions imposed by civilization on human instincts lead to a pervasive sense of dissatisfaction and psychological discomfort among individuals.

Critiques and Contemporary Views:

1. **Overemphasis on Repression:** Critics argue that Freud overemphasized the role of repression in civilization, neglecting other aspects like cooperation, empathy, and altruism that are also fundamental to societal living.

2. **Cultural Relativism:** Modern perspectives highlight that Freud's views were heavily influenced by the social and cultural context of his time and may not apply universally across different cultures and historical periods.

3. **Alternative Explanations:** Contemporary theories in psychology and sociology offer alternative explanations for the development of civilization that include economic, political, and ecological factors, in addition to psychological ones.

4. **Positive Aspects of Civilization:** While Freud focused on the tensions and conflicts arising from civilization, modern thinkers also emphasize the positive aspects of civilization, such as the security, stability, and cultural achievements it brings.

Freud's analysis of the psychological basis of civilization provides a thought-provoking perspective on the complex relationship between human nature and societal structures. It opens up avenues for exploring how individual psychological needs and societal demands interact, influencing both personal well-being and the development of civilization as a whole.

11.3. The Tension Between Individual and Society

Freud's exploration of the tension between the individual and society is a crucial aspect of his thoughts on civilization and its psychological implications. This tension highlights the complex interplay between individual desires and societal norms.

Freud's Perspective on Individual-Society Tension:

1. **Individual Desires vs. Societal Norms:** Freud posited that there is an inherent conflict between the individual's instinctual desires (especially sexual and aggressive drives) and the constraints imposed by society. While society demands restraint and conformity for collective well-being, these demands often clash with individual impulses.

2. **Role of the Superego:** The superego, which develops through the internalization of societal norms and parental values, often conflicts with the id, which seeks immediate gratification of desires. The ego mediates this conflict, but the tension can lead to internal psychic conflicts and neurosis.

3. **Societal Repression and Discontent:** Freud believed that the repression required by societal norms leads to an undercurrent of discontent among individuals. This discontent manifests in various forms of unhappiness, psychological distress, and sometimes rebellion against societal norms.

4. **Sublimation as a Coping Mechanism:** Freud saw sublimation, a process where socially unacceptable impulses are transformed into socially acceptable actions or behaviors, as a key mechanism allowing individuals to cope with this tension. Through sublimation, people find ways to express their instinctual drives creatively and acceptably.

Modern Interpretations and Critiques:

1. **Broader Socio-Psychological Dynamics:** Contemporary thinkers consider a wider range of factors influencing the individual-society relationship, including cultural, economic, and political forces.

2. **Positive Socialization Process:** Modern psychology often views the process of socialization more positively, emphasizing how societal norms and values can be internalized without necessarily leading to repression or neurosis.

3. **Diversity of Individual Experiences:** There is a greater acknowledgment of the diversity in individual experiences with societal norms, recognizing that the impact of these norms varies widely based on personal, cultural, and situational factors.

4. **Adaptive Nature of Human Behavior:** Contemporary views often focus on the adaptive nature of human behavior in response to societal pressures, highlighting resilience and the capacity for positive growth and development.

The tension between the individual and society, as conceptualized by Freud, remains a relevant and debated topic in psychology. It provides a framework for understanding various aspects of human behavior and psychological disorders within the context of societal structures and norms.

11.4. Exercise: 10 MCQs with Answers at the End

Test your understanding of Freud's views on religion, civilization, and the tension between the individual and society with these multiple-choice questions. This exercise covers the key concepts discussed in Chapter 11. Answers are provided at the end for your reference.

1. **According to Freud, religion is primarily:**

   A. A product of logical reasoning

   B. A manifestation of human wishes and desires

   C. Based on empirical evidence

   D. A reflection of societal advancement

2. **In Freud's view, the conflict between individual desires and societal norms often leads to:**

A. Economic growth

B. Neurosis

C. Improved social relationships

D. Technological advancements

3. **Freud described religion as akin to:**

A. Scientific theory

B. Universal obsessional neurosis

C. Artistic expression

D. Historical documentation

4. **The superego, according to Freud, represents:**

A. Instinctual needs and desires

B. The internalization of societal norms and values

C. The reality principle

D. Conscious thoughts and decisions

5. **Freud's theory suggests that civilization was created to:**

A. Promote individual freedom

B. Regulate human desires and impulses

C. Foster technological innovation

D. Ensure economic prosperity

6. **The concept of sublimation in Freud's theory refers to:**

A. Redirecting unacceptable impulses into socially acceptable activities

B. Denying the reality of a situation

C. Reverting to earlier stages of development

D. Projecting one's own feelings onto others

7. **According to Freud, the tension between individual and society is rooted in:**

A. Educational disparities

B. Instinctual drives and societal constraints

C. Technological advancements

D. Economic inequalities

8. **In Freudian theory, societal repression can lead to:**

A. Widespread happiness and contentment

B. An undercurrent of discontent among individuals

C. Increased creativity and innovation

D. Enhanced cognitive abilities

9. **Freud's views on religion and civilization have been critiqued for:**

A. Overemphasizing individual autonomy

B. Ignoring economic factors

C. Lack of empirical support

D. Focusing too much on technological influences

10. **Sublimation helps individuals cope with societal tensions by:**

A. Avoiding conflicts altogether

B. Transforming forbidden impulses into acceptable forms

C. Suppressing all desires and emotions

D. Enhancing personal wealth

Answers:

1. B. A manifestation of human wishes and desires

2. B. Neurosis

3. B. Universal obsessional neurosis

4. B. The internalization of societal norms and values

5. B. Regulate human desires and impulses

6. A. Redirecting unacceptable impulses into socially acceptable activities

7. B. Instinctual drives and societal constraints

8. B. An undercurrent of discontent among individuals

9. C. Lack of empirical support

10. B. Transforming forbidden impulses into acceptable forms

These questions are designed to reinforce your understanding of Freud's views on the complex relationship between individuals, society, religion, and civilization, and the psychological implications of these relationships. Reflecting on these questions can deepen your comprehension of the intricacies of Freudian theory in these areas.

Chapter 12: Freud's Later Theories

12.1. Development of Freud's Later Thoughts

Throughout his career, Sigmund Freud continually revised and expanded his theories. His later thoughts, developed towards the end of his life, demonstrate a significant evolution in his ideas, reflecting deeper insights into the human psyche.

Key Developments in Freud's Later Theories:

1. **The Death Drive (Thanatos):** One of the most significant additions to Freud's theory was the concept of the death drive, or Thanatos. This concept posited an instinctual drive towards death, self-destruction, and a return to an inorganic state. It was seen as a counterforce to Eros, the life drive, which propels individuals toward survival, growth, and creativity.

2. **Revision of the Theory of Anxiety:** Freud revised his earlier ideas about anxiety, proposing that it is more than just a result of repressed libido. He suggested that anxiety stems from an interplay of multiple internal conflicts, including the fear of external dangers and internal conflicts between the ego and the superego.

3. **Structural Model of the Psyche:** In his later work, Freud introduced a new structural model of the mind, consisting of the id, ego, and superego. This model provided a more complex understanding of the mental life and its dynamics, emphasizing the interplay between these three structures.

4. **Increased Focus on Ego Psychology:** Freud's later theories placed greater emphasis on the role and functioning of the ego. He explored how the ego mediates between the demands of the id, the constraints of the superego, and the realities of the external world.

5. **The Role of External World:** Freud began to acknowledge more explicitly the influence of social and environmental factors on psychological development. He recognized that external realities, not just internal drives, significantly impact mental health.

Impact and Reception of Later Theories:

1. **Controversy of the Death Drive:** The concept of the death drive was met with skepticism by many in the psychoanalytic community, as it was a departure from his earlier focus on sexual drives.

2. **Influence on Ego Psychology:** Freud's later emphasis on the ego laid the groundwork for the development of ego psychology, which expanded the understanding of how the ego functions in normal and pathological conditions.

3. **Foundation for Future Theories:** Freud's later thoughts provided a foundation for future psychoanalytic theories, including those that focused more on relational aspects, object relations theory, and the interplay between biology and psychology.

Freud's later theories mark an important phase in the evolution of psychoanalysis, offering a more comprehensive and nuanced view of the human mind. These ideas continue to influence contemporary psychoanalytic thought and practice, reflecting Freud's enduring impact on the field of psychology.

12.2. Revisions in Psychoanalytic Theory

Throughout his career, Freud continuously revised and refined his psychoanalytic theory, demonstrating a willingness to adapt his ideas in response to new insights and criticisms. These revisions have played a crucial role in the evolution of psychoanalytic thought.

Major Revisions in Freudian Theory:

1. **Shift from the Topographical to the Structural Model:** Freud initially conceptualized the mind in terms of the conscious, preconscious, and unconscious (topographical model). Later, he introduced the structural model (id, ego, superego), which provided a more dynamic view of the mind's internal processes and interactions.

2. **Redefining the Drives:** Freud's early work focused predominantly on the sexual drives (libido). However, later, he introduced the concept of the death drive (Thanatos), proposing a dualistic nature of human drives that included both life-preserving and destructive impulses.

3. **Anxiety Theories:** Freud's understanding of anxiety evolved over time. Initially, he associated anxiety with repressed libido. Later, he proposed that it was a response to perceived dangers and a signal of internal conflicts, particularly those involving the ego and superego.

4. **Greater Emphasis on Ego Functions:** In his later work, Freud focused more on the role of the ego. He explored how the ego functions as a mediator between internal drives, moral standards, and external reality, and its role in defense mechanisms.

5. **Acknowledgment of External Factors:** Freud's later theories acknowledged the impact of external factors, such as societal norms and cultural influences, on psychological development and functioning, moving slightly away from the exclusively internal focus of his earlier work.

Impact of These Revisions:

1. **Expanded Scope of Psychoanalysis:** These revisions broadened the scope of psychoanalysis, allowing it to address a wider range of psychological phenomena and disorders.

2. **Foundation for New Schools of Thought:** Freud's later revisions laid the groundwork for new directions in psychoanalysis, including object relations theory, ego psychology, and self-psychology.

3. **Continued Debate and Development:** Freud's willingness to revise his theories stimulated ongoing debate and development within the psychoanalytic community, contributing to the richness and diversity of psychoanalytic thought.

These revisions illustrate Freud's commitment to developing a comprehensive and coherent theoretical framework for understanding the human psyche. They reflect both the complexities of psychological phenomena and the evolving nature of psychoanalytic theory itself.

12.3. The Death Drive and Beyond

One of Freud's most intriguing and controversial later concepts is the idea of the death drive, or Thanatos. This notion marked a significant expansion of his theory beyond the earlier focus on the pleasure principle and sexual drives.

The Concept of the Death Drive (Thanatos):

1. **Definition and Nature:** Freud introduced the concept of the death drive as a fundamental force opposing Eros, the life drive. He theorized that the death drive manifests as a basic human instinct towards aggression, destruction, and a return to an inanimate state.

2. **Relationship with Eros:** The death drive is in constant opposition to Eros, which drives individuals towards survival, procreation, and creativity. Freud saw human behavior as a result of the interplay between these two drives.

3. **Manifestation in Behavior:** The death drive was thought to manifest in behaviors such as aggression, self-destructiveness, and certain manifestations of masochism. Freud also linked it to the compulsion to repeat earlier traumatic events or negative experiences.

Beyond the Death Drive: Evolutions in Freud's Thought:

1. **Civilization's Discontents:** In his later work, "Civilization and Its Discontents," Freud explored how the tension between individual instincts (including the death drive) and societal norms leads to a sense of chronic unhappiness and psychological conflict.

2. **Application in Therapy:** The concept of the death drive has been used to understand and treat certain types of neuroses and behaviors, particularly those involving self-destructive patterns and aggression.

3. **Criticism and Debate:** The death drive theory has been one of the most debated aspects of Freud's work. Critics argue that it lacks empirical support and is too abstract to be useful. Others interpret the concept more metaphorically, seeing it as a way of understanding self-destructive tendencies and the repetitive nature of certain psychological patterns.

4. **Influence on Later Theories:** Despite its controversial nature, the concept of the death drive influenced later psychoanalytic theories, particularly in understanding aggression and destructive behavior. It also sparked discussions in areas beyond psychology, including philosophy, cultural studies, and literary criticism.

The introduction of the death drive represents Freud's continued efforts to deepen and complexify his understanding of human psychology. It highlights his willingness to explore the darker, less understood aspects of the human psyche and has contributed to a more nuanced understanding of human behavior and mental processes.

12.4. Exercise: 10 MCQs with Answers at the End

Test your understanding of the developments in Freud's later theories with these multiple-choice questions. This exercise covers the concepts discussed in Chapter 12, focusing on the evolution of Freud's thought, including the death drive and changes in his psychoanalytic theory. Answers are provided at the end for your reference.

1. Freud's later theory introduced the concept of the death drive, also known as:

A. Eros

B. Thanatos

C. Libido

D. Superego

2. In Freud's structural model of the psyche, which element is responsible for mediating between the id, superego, and reality?

A. The ego

B. The id

C. The superego

D. The libido

3. Which of the following best describes Freud's death drive?

A. The instinct towards life and creativity

B. The drive towards aggression and self-destruction

C. The desire for sexual fulfillment

D. The need for societal approval

4. **Freud's revised theory of anxiety suggests that it arises from:**

A. Only external factors

B. The conflict between the ego and reality

C. Unfulfilled sexual desires

D. The imbalance of biological chemicals

5. **Which Freudian concept reflects the tension between societal norms and individual desires?**

A. Oedipus complex

B. Repression

C. Civilization's discontents

D. Dream symbolism

6. **In his later works, Freud placed greater emphasis on:**

A. The role of the id

B. The sexual drives in childhood

C. The functioning of the ego

D. The influence of the superego

7. **Freud's concept of the death drive was met with:**

A. Universal acceptance

B. Skepticism and controversy

C. Indifference by the psychoanalytic community

D. Immediate empirical validation

8. According to Freud's later theories, what role does the superego play?

A. It serves as the source of sexual energy

B. It mediates between desires and moral restrictions

C. It is responsible for conscious thought processes

D. It governs instinctual drives

9. Freud's late work 'Civilization and Its Discontents' deals with:

A. The development of artistic abilities

B. The impact of culture on personality

C. The psychological tension between civilization and individual instincts

D. Techniques in dream analysis

10. Freud's structural model of the psyche includes:

A. Id, Ego, and Superego

B. Conscious, Unconscious, and Preconscious

C. Libido, Thanatos, and Eros

D. Oedipus complex, Electra complex, and Neurosis

Answers:

1. B. Thanatos

2. A. The ego

3. B. The drive towards aggression and self-destruction

4. B. The conflict between the ego and reality

5. C. Civilization's discontents

6. C. The functioning of the ego

7. B. Skepticism and controversy

8. B. It mediates between desires and moral restrictions

9. C. The psychological tension between civilization and individual instincts

10. A. Id, Ego, and Superego

These questions are designed to reinforce your understanding of the later developments in Freud's psychoanalytic theory, including his conceptualization of the death drive and the evolution of his ideas on the psyche's structure and anxiety. Reflecting on these questions can deepen your comprehension of these advanced aspects of Freudian theory.

Chapter 13: The Legacy and Evolution of Freudian Psychology

13.1. Reappraisal of Freud in Modern Psychology

The impact of Sigmund Freud on psychology is undeniable, though his work has been subject to extensive reappraisal and debate in modern psychological thought. While some of his ideas have been revised or rejected, many continue to influence contemporary psychology and psychotherapy.

Key Areas of Reappraisal:

1. **Empirical Validation:** One of the main criticisms of Freud's work is the lack of empirical evidence for many of his theories. Modern psychology, with its emphasis on empirical methods and evidence-based practices, has questioned and tested many of Freud's hypotheses.

2. **Cultural and Historical Context:** Contemporary psychologists acknowledge that Freud's theories were influenced by the cultural and historical context of his time. This has led to a

reevaluation of his work, considering the societal norms and scientific knowledge of the early 20th century.

3. **The Unconscious Mind:** Freud's concept of the unconscious mind remains a significant contribution. Modern psychology and neuroscience have continued to explore the unconscious, though often in different terms and with more empirical approaches.

4. **Psychosexual Development:** While Freud's stages of psychosexual development have been largely critiqued, the idea that early childhood experiences can significantly impact adult personality and behavior is a lasting contribution.

5. **Defense Mechanisms:** Freud's identification and description of defense mechanisms are still relevant in modern psychology. Concepts like repression, projection, and sublimation are frequently used in various forms of psychotherapy.

6. **Therapeutic Techniques:** Techniques such as free association and the interpretation of dreams still have a place in psychotherapy, particularly in psychodynamic approaches.

Modern Perspectives on Freud's Legacy:

1. **Integration with New Theories:** Freud's theories have been integrated with new psychological models and research. For instance, attachment theory and object relations theory have incorporated and expanded upon Freudian ideas.

2. **Psychodynamic Therapy:** Modern psychodynamic therapy, while evolving from Freudian psychoanalysis, has adapted to include a more relational approach, a focus on the therapeutic alliance, and an integration of newer psychological research.

3. **Influence Beyond Psychology:** Freud's work continues to influence fields beyond psychology, including literature, art, and cultural studies, where his theories are used to explore and interpret human behavior and cultural phenomena.

4. **Ongoing Debate:** Freud remains a polarizing figure in psychology. His theories continue to spark debate, prompting ongoing discussion and critical examination within the field.

Freud's work, despite its controversies, laid the groundwork for much of modern psychological thought. His ideas have sparked extensive research and discussion, leading to a deeper understanding of the human mind and behavior. The reappraisal of Freud in modern psychology reflects the field's evolution and the enduring relevance of his pioneering work.

13.2. The Influence on Psychotherapy and Psychiatry

Sigmund Freud's influence on psychotherapy and psychiatry is monumental, shaping the way mental health is understood and treated. Despite various criticisms and evolutions in the field, many of his concepts and methods remain foundational in contemporary practice.

Key Influences of Freudian Psychology on Psychotherapy and Psychiatry:

1. **The Therapeutic Process:** Freud's development of the talking cure laid the foundation for modern psychotherapy. The importance he placed on talking as a way of exploring and resolving psychological issues is central to most therapeutic approaches today.

2. **Unconscious Processes:** Freud's focus on the unconscious mind revolutionized the understanding of human behavior and mental disorders. The concept that much of our mental life is unconscious is now widely accepted and forms the basis of numerous therapeutic techniques.

3. **Defense Mechanisms:** Freud's identification of defense mechanisms such as repression, projection, and denial has been integral in understanding how individuals cope with stress and trauma. These concepts are routinely employed in therapeutic settings.

4. **Transference and Countertransference:** Freud's exploration of transference and countertransference dynamics in therapy has profoundly influenced clinical practice. Understanding these phenomena is crucial in therapeutic relationships and in managing the emotional interaction between therapists and their clients.

5. **Childhood Experiences and Development:** Freud's emphasis on early childhood experiences in shaping personality and potential mental health issues later in life has been a significant contribution. This has led to a greater focus on child and adolescent psychotherapy and the importance of early interventions.

6. **Psychoanalytic Techniques:** While traditional psychoanalysis is less common now, many of its techniques, such as dream analysis and free association, have been adapted and are still used in various forms of psychodynamic therapy.

7. **Influence on Psychiatric Diagnosis:** Freud's work influenced the understanding of various mental disorders, from anxiety and depression to more complex conditions like hysteria (now understood as conversion and dissociative disorders).

Contemporary Adaptations:

1. **Integration with Other Approaches:** Modern psychotherapy often integrates Freudian concepts with other approaches, including cognitive-behavioral therapy (CBT), humanistic psychology, and systemic family therapy.

2. **Reinterpretation of Concepts:** Some of Freud's ideas have been reinterpreted or modified in light of new research in psychology, neuroscience, and related fields.

3. **Diverse Therapeutic Applications:** Freudian concepts are applied in diverse therapeutic contexts, from individual therapy to group settings, and in addressing a wide range of psychological issues.

Freud's influence on psychotherapy and psychiatry is enduring. His pioneering work laid the groundwork for understanding the complexities of the human mind and continues to inspire and challenge mental health professionals in their practice and research.

13.3. Freud's Enduring Impact

Sigmund Freud's impact on psychology, psychotherapy, and broader cultural understanding of the human psyche is enduring and multifaceted. Despite various criticisms and the evolution of psychological theories, Freud's foundational concepts continue to influence and provoke thought in multiple disciplines.

Areas of Freud's Enduring Impact:

1. **Understanding of the Unconscious:** Freud's exploration of the unconscious mind revolutionized psychology. The idea that much of our mental life is beyond conscious awareness is a concept that continues to influence both clinical practice and theoretical psychology.

2. **Psychotherapy and Counseling:** Freud's development of psychoanalytic therapy laid the groundwork for modern psychotherapy. Techniques like free association, dream analysis, and the exploration of childhood experiences are still used, in varied forms, in psychotherapy today.

3. **Language and Culture:** Freud introduced terms such as "ego," "id," "superego," and "Freudian slip" that have become ingrained in everyday language and culture. His ideas have permeated literature, art, film, and popular media, influencing how we interpret human behavior and motivations.

4. **Child Development and Education:** Freud's emphasis on early childhood as a critical period for psychological development has had a lasting effect on education and child psychology, highlighting the importance of early experiences and the developmental environment.

5. **Impact on Other Disciplines:** Freud's theories have had a significant influence on various fields, including sociology, anthropology, literature, and philosophy, sparking new ways of thinking about culture, society, and human nature.

6. **Critical Thought and Debate:** Freud's work continues to be a source of critical thought and debate. It challenges psychologists, therapists, and scholars to consider the complexities of the human psyche and the myriad factors that influence behavior and mental processes.

7. **Evolution of Psychoanalysis:** Freud's theories have evolved into various schools of psychoanalytic thought, such as object relations theory, ego psychology, and relational psychoanalysis, each building upon and expanding his original ideas.

Modern Relevance:

While some of Freud's theories have been revised or critiqued in light of new scientific findings and societal changes, the core principles of his work retain relevance. They continue to provide valuable insights into understanding the human mind and behavior, and the complexities of mental health. Freud's legacy is evident in the ongoing exploration and dialogue about the depths of human psychology, demonstrating the lasting impact of his work.

13.4. Exercise: 10 MCQs with Answers at the End

Test your knowledge of the legacy and evolution of Freudian psychology with these multiple-choice questions. This exercise covers the key concepts discussed in Chapter 13. Answers are provided at the end for your reference.

1. **Freud's concept of the unconscious has primarily influenced:**

   A. Neurosurgery

   B. Modern psychotherapy

C. Computer programming

D. Urban planning

2. In contemporary psychotherapy, Freud's techniques such as dream analysis and free association are:

A. Completely abandoned

B. Used in their original form

C. Adapted and integrated into various therapeutic approaches

D. Only used in psychoanalysis

3. Freud's ideas have permeated popular culture and are evident in:

A. Financial modeling

B. Everyday language and media

C. Physics theories

D. Culinary arts

4. Freud's emphasis on early childhood experiences influenced:

A. Astrophysics

B. Child psychology and education

C. Political science

D. Engineering

5. **Which field has NOT been significantly influenced by Freud's theories?**

A. Sociology

B. Literature

C. Mathematics

D. Philosophy

6. **Freud's work continues to provoke:**

A. Uniform acceptance

B. Critical thought and debate

C. Indifference

D. Scientific experimentation

7. **Freud's exploration of the unconscious mind contributed to the development of:**

A. Quantum mechanics

B. Cognitive behavioral therapy

C. Psychodynamic therapy

D. Structural engineering

8. **One of the criticisms of Freud's theories in modern psychology is their:**

A. Overemphasis on empirical evidence

B. Lack of scientific support and empirical validation

C. Focus on artificial intelligence

D. Emphasis on environmental factors

9. Freud's influence on child development emphasized the importance of:

A. Early childhood experiences

B. Genetic factors

C. Peer influence in adolescence

D. Technological advancements in education

10. Freud's work has been influential in the field of:

A. Geology

B. Anthropology

C. Astronomy

D. Mechanical engineering

Answers:

1. B. Modern psychotherapy

2. C. Adapted and integrated into various therapeutic approaches

3. B. Everyday language and media

4. B. Child psychology and education

5. C. Mathematics

6. B. Critical thought and debate

7. C. Psychodynamic therapy

8. B. Lack of scientific support and empirical validation

9. A. Early childhood experiences

10. B. Anthropology

These questions are designed to reinforce your understanding of Freud's lasting impact on various aspects of psychology, psychotherapy, and culture, as well as the ongoing debates and critiques of his work. Reflecting on these questions can deepen your comprehension of the complexities and enduring relevance of Freudian psychology.

Conclusion

As we conclude our exploration of Freudian psychology, it's clear that Sigmund Freud's contributions have profoundly shaped our understanding of the human mind. His theories on the unconscious, defense mechanisms, psychosexual development, and the dynamics of the psyche have been pivotal in the evolution of psychotherapy and psychology. Despite the controversies and criticisms, Freud's work remains a cornerstone in the field, continuing to influence and inspire ongoing research and practice.

Key Takeaways:

1. **Foundational Theories:** Freud's concepts of the unconscious, the id, ego, and superego, and his exploration of defense mechanisms and psychosexual development, form the bedrock of psychoanalytic thought.

2. **Evolution and Adaptation:** Freud's theories have evolved and been adapted over time, reflecting changes in scientific understanding and cultural contexts.

3. **Influence Across Disciplines:** Freud's ideas have extended beyond psychology, impacting fields like literature, art, sociology, and cultural studies.

4. **Enduring Legacy:** Despite criticisms, Freud's work continues to be a source of insight and debate, contributing to our deeper understanding of human behavior and mental processes.

5. **Contemporary Relevance:** Modern psychotherapy and psychiatry still draw on Freudian concepts, integrating them with new theories and approaches.

Freud's legacy is a testament to the complexity and depth of human psychology. His pioneering work opened avenues for exploring the depths of the human psyche and laid the foundation for much of the psychological thought and practice we see today. As we continue to advance in our understanding of the mind, Freud's work remains a critical reference point, reminding us of the intricate and often hidden forces that shape human behavior.

The best way to thank an author is to write a review.